The Men Who Made
the Yankees

Also by W. Nikola-Lisa

The Men Who Made the Yankees

W. Nikola-Lisa

Gyroscope Books
Chicago

Y M
796.357
Nik

PUBLISHED BY GYROSCOPE BOOKS
gyroscopebooks.com

Published in the United States by Gyroscope Books, a Chicago-based
publisher of high quality hardback, paperback and digital books for
readers young and old.

Book design by Tom Greensfelder.

Author: Nikola-Lisa, W. [American, b.1951]
Summary: A history of the New York Yankees beginning with the
rise of the American League in the mid-1890s to the Yankees' first
World Series championship title in 1923.

Library of Congress Control Number: 2014910361
Gyroscope Books, Chicago, IL

ISBN: 978-0-9972524-0-8

Printed in the United States

TABLE OF CONTENTS

Newly acquired slugger George Herman ("Babe") Ruth stands arms akimbo on the steps of the New York Yankees dugout.

EVERY SCHOOL KID looks forward to the end of the school year. I certainly did. I grew up in Texas and Florida, but my mother's family was from Jersey City. At the end of the school year, my mother, a single parent, shipped my sisters and me north, to my grandmother's beach house on Staten Island.

Wedged between New Dorp and Great Kills Harbor, Cedar Grove Beach Club was a gated beachfront community, rare for its time, an idyll among the surrounding working-class communities. It was here that I spent the summers of my childhood under the watchful eye of my mother's sister Betty and her husband Fred.

Uncle Fred loved the beach. He loved digging for clams, tooling around in his speedboat, playing cards at the clubhouse, and, of course, chatting with friends over drinks on the front porch.

Occasionally, he'd corral a couple of tickets to a New York Yankees' game and off we'd go, just the two of us, to historic Yankee Stadium.

Thus started my fascination with major league baseball and the New York Yankees. It was the early 1960s and I had the good fortune to watch some of the best players of the era: Whitey Ford, Ralph Terry, Clete Boyer, Elston Howard, and Mickey Mantle.

Over the years fascination turned into curiosity, and I began researching the origin of the Yankee franchise. What struck me the most about their story was the fact that it was not one man, or two, but several men—often friends, but just as often adversaries—who were responsible for the formation of the Yankee franchise, today one of the most successful ball clubs in major league baseball. *–W.N.-L.*

Baseball is a man maker.
Al Spalding

CHAPTER ONE

Ghosts from the Past

ON NOVEMBER 18, 1893, Ban Johnson, sports editor for the *Cincinnati Commercial-Gazette*, accepted the presidency of the Western League, a small minor league operating in the Midwest. The league, which was teetering on bankruptcy, had teams in Toledo, Indianapolis, Sioux City, Milwaukee, Minneapolis, Kansas City, and Grand Rapids. In the grand scheme of things it was an unimportant minor league circuit, but Johnson, a strong-willed, forceful man, had plans to make it one of the best leagues in the country.

Johnson's vision was bolstered by his belief that in order for organized baseball to appeal to the widest audience it had to be clean: free from cheating, profanity, and rowdy behavior. Professional baseball in the 1890s was

Photo: Opening Day, Yankee Stadium, April 18, 1923. Left to right: Jake Ruppert, co-owner, New York Yankees; Kenesaw Mountain Landis, newly-appointed Commissioner of Baseball; and T. L. Huston, co-owner, New York Yankees.

far from that. It was not unusual during the course of a game to see managers jostling umpires, players brawling on the infield, or fans pummeling each other in the stands. Johnson was determined to clean up the sport.

Professional baseball began in the 1860s when the prevailing amateur association allowed players to be paid. One of those players was Harry Wright, the player-manager of the Cincinnati Red Stockings, who put ten players, including his brother, on salary for the 1869 season. But not every team in the loosely structured association did the same. When the league went belly-up after the 1870 season, Wright moved to Boston and helped form the first all-professional baseball league, which was named The National Association of Professional Base Ball Players.

From the start, however, the National Association faltered. The reasons were several. First of all, there was no advanced scheduling. Each team merely promised to play all of the others at least five times before the season ended at the beginning of November. Secondly, although players were contractually bound to a team during the season, as soon as the season ended players often jumped to another team, lured by the promise of more money. And, third, since the entry fee to join the National Association was a modest $10, many weak teams simply dropped out in the middle of the season if they were unable to meet their payroll.

For these reasons, over the five years the National

Association existed, only three teams—Boston, Philadelphia and New York—played all five seasons. The constant upheaval was too much for the association, and by 1875 some of its owners were looking for a new kind of organization.

A League of Club Owners

One of the team owners was William Ambrose Hulbert who ran the National Association's Chicago franchise. Hulbert, a wealthy coal merchant, understood that there was money to be made in major league baseball, but not under the current organization. Instead of a loose organization of players, Hulbert believed what was needed was an association of tight-fisted club owners. As soon as the 1875 season ended, Hulbert began to talk with other club owners, including former owners who wanted to get back into organized baseball.

IN THE EARLY DAYS of professional baseball, club owners issued contracts to players on a year-to-year basis. This meant that at the end of a season players could jump to another team that offered them more money. To keep salaries from continually escalating, and to retain their most valuable players, in 1879 club owners instituted the reserve clause (also known as "the five man rule"), which allowed teams to "reserve" up to five players for the coming season. The only way a player could opt out of his contract was to refrain from playing in the league for a full year. The reserve clause not only kept player salaries from escalating, but it also gave club owners an all-powerful tool: they could retain their most valuable players through the clause, trade them to other teams for the rights of other players, or sell them outright for cash.

Hulbert was motivated to act not only out of his conviction that a new form of management was necessary to keep professional baseball thriving, but also out of self-interest. At the end of the 1875 season, Hulbert raided two National Association teams, enticing some of their best players to sign contracts with his Chicago team.

Rather than wait to see if club owners in the National Association would expel him for his actions, Hulbert convinced a handful of current and former club owners of the National Association to form a new organization, which would put the control of major league baseball—both on and off the field—in the hands of franchise owners.

The decisive meeting occurred on February 2, 1876, at the Grand Central Hotel in New York. At the meeting Hulbert stressed several key principles that led to the formation of the National League of Professional Base Ball Clubs.

> ✦ The National League would be a league of club owners, and not a loose organization of players.
> ✦ League membership would be limited to clubs in cities with populations of 75,000 or more that paid a $100 entry fee (a tenfold increase over the National Association's entry fee).
> ✦ All player contracts would be written and enforced.
> ✦ Ticket prices would be set at fifty cents per person.
> ✦ No ballgames would be played on Sunday.

In addition to these guidelines, gambling at ballgames was strictly forbidden, as was the serving of alcoholic beverages. Moreover, players were forbidden to drink both on and off the field. Any player who broke the league's rules or their team's rules ran the risk of being banned from playing or "blacklisted" by the league for life.

The meeting ended with the writing of a constitution outlining these and other regulations that distinguished the National League from its predecessor. At the conclusion of the meeting, Hulbert, echoing the prevailing business model of the late 19th century, reminded those present that club owners should do everything within their power to stamp out challenges to their authority.

Like any new endeavor, the first few years of operation were fraught with turmoil. The league opened the 1876 season with teams in Boston, Chicago, Cincinnati, St. Louis, Harford, Connecticut, New York, Philadelphia, and Louisville. But it wasn't long before two teams—Cincinnati and Hartford—fell into financial difficulties. Hulbert's headache was compounded by the expulsion of New York and Philadelphia at the end of the 1877 season for conspiring with gamblers to throw the pennant race to Boston.

CHARTER MEMBERS OF THE NATIONAL LEAGUE

Boston Red Stockings
Chicago White Stockings
Cincinnati Red Stockings
Hartford Dark Blues
Louisville Grays
New York Mutuals
Philadelphia Athletics
St. Louis Brown Stockings

By the beginning of the 1878 season, five of the original eight teams—Louisville, Hartford, St. Louis,

New York, and Philadelphia—had folded, and two of Hulbert's replacement teams—Indianapolis and Milwaukee—were floundering. Miraculously, however, the National League rebounded, led by a strong Providence, Rhode Island team. The stability was short-lived however when Hulbert died suddenly in the spring of 1882 and the league found itself not only without a leader, but also with its first outside challenge.

A Bitter War

One effect the ever-changing membership of teams had on the National League was that it left as many owners outside of the league as it did inside of it. Several of these former team owners decided that the time was right to launch a second major league to challenge the dominance of the National League.

The precipitating event occurred at the beginning of the 1881 season, a year before Hulbert's death, when Hulbert expelled Cincinnati from the National League for insisting that it sell beer at its home games. The outrage over the action reverberated throughout professional baseball, especially in Cincinnati and St. Louis, both big beer-brewing cities. At first the two cities decided to field their own independent teams—the Cincinnati Reds and the St. Louis Browns—that would play each other in regular competition.

But as 1882 neared, it became evident that there were other parties just as interested in hosting major league baseball teams. So, Oliver Caylor, sports editor for the *Cincinnati Enquirer*, and Justus Thorner, president of the former National League team in Cincinnati, teamed up with Alfred Spink, a baseball promoter in St. Louis, Chris von der Ahe, an associate of Spink's who owned a beer garden across the street from Sportsman's Park in St. Louis where the Browns played, and Pittsburgh businessman Denny McNight, an iron manufacturer, to form the American Association.

Three things distinguished the American Association from the National League: the sale of liquor at ballgames, Sunday afternoon baseball, and half-price tickets. American Association teams took the field for the 1882 season in six cities: Cincinnati, St. Louis, Louisville, Pittsburgh, Philadelphia, and Baltimore.

Owners of National League teams were furious, calling the new organization "the Beer-and-Whiskey League." They were angriest over the fact that in order for American Association clubs to stock their teams, they had to steal many of their players from the National League. They did this by ignoring the National League's reserve clause, which bound a player to a team even after his yearly contract had expired.

American Association owners saw no reason to abide by a clause they did not write. So early in the spring of 1882 they went hunting for as many

National League players as they could lure away. The bitter war lasted until the following year when the two sides sat down and worked out a compromise. The settlement, called the National Agreement of 1883, put an end to the raids. The two sides agreed to honor each other's contracts, including the reserve clause. They also agreed to observe the blacklist, which meant that owners maintained control over the game and the lives of their players.

THE NATIONAL AGREEMENT (also known as the Tripartite Agreement) was drafted on February 17, 1883, at a meeting in New York between the National League and the American Association. The Agreement, also signed by the Northwestern League, a minor league circuit, put an end to player raids by protecting each team's player contracts. The reserve clause was also amended to allow each team to reserve up to eleven players, more than doubling the amount of players that teams were able to reserve under the original 1879 agreement.

Doomed From the Start

The peace the two sides sought, however, was shattered within a year when yet another major league formed. The league was known as the Union Association, the brainchild of Henry Lucas, a St. Louis realtor who had fallen in love with the game ever since his brother had run the National League's St. Louis team in 1877. To gain a foothold in territory where there were already two leagues meant that Lucas needed an angle, something that would not only attract backers, but also players.

He found one.

Lucas railed against the reserve clause, saying that players were unjustly treated because of it. This got the players attention, and it gained several important backers for Lucas' cause, including Adolphus Busch, who ran a brewery in St. Louis. But the very thing that Lucas professed to loathe became the reason the proposed league failed.

Without a reserve clause baseball clubs were free to go after the best talent available. This was well and good, if a team had the money to do so. However, teams without a large bankroll suffered by losing all of their best players to the richest teams. And this is precisely what happened to Lucas' Union Association.

The St. Louis Maroons, by far the league's wealthiest team, purchased the best players in the league and went on to decimate their competition during the 1884 season, winning the Union Association's pennant with a lopsided record of 94 wins and 19 losses. The result was that fans lost interest in the pennant race early in the season and stopped coming to the games. Doomed from the start, the Union Association folded at the end of the season.

The other two leagues also felt the effects of the breakup of the Union Association. First of all, in order to fight the proposed third league, the National League convinced the American Association to expand from eight teams to twelve. The two leagues conspired to battle the Union Association by placing either a National League or an American Association team in every Union Association city. After the Union Association folded, the National League had little adjusting to do, as they held firm in most of their cities, dropping only its Cleveland franchise (replacing it, much to the resentment of American Association owners, with the Union Association's St. Louis franchise).

The American Association, on the other hand, had a bloated twelve-team structure, which it could not afford to keep afloat. So, at the end of the 1884 season, it cut franchises in Washington, Indianapolis, Columbus, and Toledo. This act, along with the disintegration of the Union League, ushered in a brief period of calm.

But it did not last.

Revolt from Within

Missing in all of the owners' calculations were considerations for players. Ever since the institution of the blacklist and the reserve clause, players balked at the control team owners held over them. But team owners were deaf to players' concerns, and continued to heap other restrictive practices on top of these offensives. Most of the practices had to do with restricting player behavior or limiting their salary. Although a minimum salary of $1,000 had been established in 1883, a salary cap of $2,400 soon followed. This enraged players who saw their salaries frozen while club owners' profits soared. The whole affair came to a head at the end of the 1888 season.

Albert Spalding, who succeeded Hulbert as the president of the National League's Chicago White Stockings, organized a series of exhibition games for members of the White Stockings and an all-star group of American Association players that would take them around the world. They played baseball on the coast of Australia, in the shade of Egypt's pyramids, in the manicured Borghese Gardens in Rome, and beneath a looming Eiffel Tower.

It was a fine tour, except that while they were gone John Brush, who owned the National League's Cincinnati franchise, proposed that the entire structure of player salaries be revamped. Brush argued that players should be paid according to their ability and their level of intensity. He proposed a graduated pay scale that ranged from $1,500 for Class E players to $2,500 for Class A players.

ALBERT GOODWILL SPALDING began his baseball career in Illinois, pitching for the Rockford Forest Citys. He went on to play for William Hulbert's Chicago Excelsiors, and then for Harry Wright's Boston Red Stockings. Spalding became a national figure while playing in Boston, leading the Red Stockings to four consecutive championships. Known as "Big Al," Spalding dominated the pitching mound. He won 57 games in one year, 24 of them in a row, and was the first pitcher to win more than 200 career games. In 1874, Hulbert enticed Spalding back to Chicago to play for and manage Hulbert's Chicago White Stockings. It was in Chicago that Spalding made his mark—as player, manager, club owner, and eventually league president. But his real influence was in the area of baseball equipment, founding one of the most successful sporting goods manufacturing businesses.

Players were outraged. Their spokesman, John Montgomery Ward, who had gone on Spalding's worldwide barnstorming tour, spoke out vigorously against the proposal. But National League owners, who had already approved the proposal, held firm. When they refused to let Ward raise the issue at an owners' meeting, players began to meet secretly to discuss their options. They already had a mechanism for doing so, thanks to Ward who had formed the Brotherhood of Professional Base Ball Players several years earlier in order to fight the suffocating reserve clause and dreaded blacklist.

When owners of the National League got wind of the players' secret meetings, they tightened the screws even further, making an absolute salary cap of $2,500 and charging players for the rental of their uniforms. This final insult put players over the top and they poured all of their energies into forming a third major league, the Players League. By 1890, they were ready. The Players League, having signed seventy National League and sixteen American Association players, fielded teams in every National League city, except Cincinnati. Moreover, they successfully enlisted many of the National League's most famous players.

Although the real war was between the Players League and the National League, which had continued to put into practice restrictive player regulations, by the end of the 1890 season all three leagues felt the loss of gate receipts.

Spalding, the most influential owner at the time, decided that something had to be done. With the support of National League owners, Spalding demanded that players who played for the Players League return to their old teams. If they did not, and the Players League failed, they would be banned from the sport for life. The bluff worked, and it was a bluff for the truth of the matter was that the National League was reeling just as badly from the loss of gate receipts as the other two leagues.

After a peace settlement was worked out, the Players League was disbanded and players were allowed—without penalty—to return to their former National League or American Association team. Most importantly, at least for players, Brush's classification scheme for allotting player salaries was abandoned, although the $2,500 salary cap was retained.

Picking Up the Pieces

The residue of the failed Players League was felt both by the National League and the American Association, but more by the American Association that had less solid financial backing than the National League. Although they tried to continue, their twenty-five cent admission charge was not enough to cover soaring operation expenses. By the end of the 1891 season, they were forced to disband.

The National League stepped into the chaos, not to help the American Association, but to pick up the pieces. It invited four American Association teams—St. Louis, Louisville, Baltimore, and Washington—to join the National League. In doing so, the league finally got what it had wanted all along: a monopoly over professional major league baseball. The twelve-team league, which settled on a 154-game regular season schedule, consisted of teams in St. Louis, Chicago, Cincinnati, Cleveland, Louisville, Pittsburgh, Philadelphia, Baltimore, Washington, New York, Brooklyn, and Boston.

It was against this backdrop that the strong-willed, cigar-smoking Ban Johnson accepted the presidency of the Western League.

A good umpire is the umpire you don't even notice.
Ban Johnson

CHAPTER TWO

Waiting in the Wings

BYRON BANCROFT ("BAN") Johnson was the son of an Ohio college professor. Born in Norwalk, Ohio, in 1865, Johnson attended Marietta College where he played baseball on the school's varsity team. Johnson was a big man who weighed close to 200 pounds; he was also quick, energetic, and ambitious.

Johnson left college early to pursue a career as a reporter. The *Cincinnati Commercial-Gazette* hired him to cover sporting events. Johnson, a sports enthusiast, enjoyed the work and quickly climbed the ranks, from cub reporter to sports page editor, where he had plenty of latitude in his editorials. His favorite target was John Brush, who owned two baseball clubs: the major league Cincinnati Reds of the National League and the minor league Indianapolis Hoosiers of the Western League. Johnson was often critical of how Brush moved players between teams. Brush, an Indianapolis department store magnate, was not one to sit back and take criticism, especially from an upstart sports editor, and he often complained publicly of Johnson's prickly editorials. Before the friction between the two men erupted into a public display of anger, Brush found a convenient way to get rid of Johnson. The opportunity arose in 1893 when Johnson's name surfaced as a possible candidate for president of the Western League. Ironically, it was Brush's Cincinnati manager, Charles Comiskey, who recommended Johnson for the position. In the tight circle of Cincinnati baseball enthusiasts, Johnson and Comiskey had become good friends and drinking buddies.

Instead of blocking Johnson's candidacy, Brush tacitly approved it by conveniently missing his train to the Western League's annual meeting. Without Brush to block Johnson's candidacy, League owners overwhelmingly voted Johnson the Western League's new president.

A Thorn in His Side

In his first year of office, Johnson found himself in the midst of a major league baseball feud. After the National League expanded to a twelve-team league in 1891, rumors of a revived American Association surfaced. The rumors worried Johnson because he knew how the new league planned to stock its teams: they would raid the minor leagues of their best players.

In order to prevent owners of the revived American Association from raiding Western League teams, Johnson sought the protection of the National League, even though Johnson was not sympathetic to the stranglehold the organization had on the major leagues. In the end, the rumors of a renewed American Association faded, and a second major league never materialized.

Although Johnson should have been on good terms with National League owners, he wasn't because he continued to irritate Cincinnati Reds' owner John Brush. What angered Johnson the most was Brush's habit of buying minor league players from other Western League teams with the intent of sending them to his major league club in Cincinnati, which he had every right to do under the agreement signed by the major and minor leagues. However, more often than not, the players wound up playing for Brush's Western League franchise in Indianapolis before being shipped off to Cincinnati to play in the major leagues.

CINCINNATI HAS THE DISTINCTION
of hosting the first all-professional team, the
Cincinnati Red Stockings, under the leadership of
Harry and George Wright. Founded at the height
of the Civil War, in 1863, the Red Stockings
turned professional in 1869. Then, for the next
two seasons, the club went undefeated, winning
130 games in a row before being beaten by the
Brooklyn Atlantics in a thrilling 11-inning game
at the Atlantic's Capitoline Grounds ballpark.

Although minor league owners frowned upon the tactic, it worked exceedingly well for Brush and other National League owners who regularly did the same. In Brush's case, the success of this tactic was evident: his Indianapolis Hoosiers dominated the Western League from 1895 to 1899, winning three out of five championship titles.

Johnson, however, didn't just sit on his hands hoping Brush would disappear. He complained repeatedly to National League officials of Brush's underhanded tactics. Finally, the National League's Board of Arbitration sided with Johnson, and Brush was forced to sell his interest in the Indianapolis franchise.

With Brush out of the picture, Johnson continued to consolidate power. He did this by finding baseball enthusiasts who shared his vision of organized baseball. One of these men was his good friend and drinking buddy Charles Comiskey. After Brush fired Comiskey at the end of the 1894 season, Johnson promptly offered him the Western League's Sioux City ball club, helping him relocate the ailing franchise to St. Paul, Minnesota, an emerging baseball city.

CHARLES ALBERT ("OLD ROMAN") COMISKEY was a major league player, team manager, and club owner. Comiskey began his professional baseball career with the St. Louis Brown Stockings, a member of the American Association, joining the team in 1882. Soon he became the Browns' player-manager, and within a few years its full-time manager. Under his leadership, Comiskey led the Browns to four consecutive American Association championships.

Leaving the Browns after the 1889 season, Comiskey bounced from team to team looking for another managerial challenge: he managed the Chicago Pirates in 1890, returned to St. Louis to manage the Browns in 1891, then managed John Brush's Cincinnati Red Stockings from 1892 to 1894.

It was while in Cincinnati that Comiskey met Ban Johnson, sports editor for the Cincinnati Commercial-Gazette. After Brush fired Comiskey at the end of the 1894 season, Johnson, who was now president of the Western

League, convinced Comiskey to purchase the Western League's Sioux City club and move it to St. Paul, Minnesota.

After several successful years in St. Paul as the club's owner-manager, Comiskey, again at Johnson's urging, moved the St. Paul club to Chicago before the start of the 1900 season. Comiskey's Chicago White Stockings (later shortened to White Sox) played on the south side of Chicago, one of eight franchises in Johnson's expanding empire.

Another one of Johnson's earliest supporters was Cornelius McGillicuddy, known in baseball circles as Connie Mack. When Mack quit the National League's Pittsburgh team in 1897, Johnson offered him the Western League's Milwaukee franchise. Although Johnson didn't know it then, both Comiskey and Mack would become two of the most successful major league franchise owners of their day.

By the end of the 1897 season, Johnson had teams in Indianapolis, Detroit, Columbus, Milwaukee, Kansas City, Buffalo, Minneapolis, and St. Paul. But Johnson wasn't through. He was ready for the next step, a step aided—quite unintentionally—by the National League.

Syndicate Baseball

While Johnson was strengthening the Western League, owners of National League teams were facing an ever-growing problem of their own. By 1897, more than half of the owners of National League teams owned an interest in more than one ball club. Like Brush, owners shuffled players from one team to another, depending upon their need at the time. Although owners considered the practice as a way to strengthen teams in emerging baseball markets, the press condemned it as "syndicate baseball," saying that it undermined fan interest and hurt organized baseball in the long run.

The most flagrant case of syndicate baseball involved Frank Robison who owned two National League teams: the St. Louis Perfectos and the Cleveland Spiders. When city officials in Cleveland announced that they would not allow Robison to expand the Spider's weekly schedule to include Sunday ballgames, Robison decided to move the heart of the Cleveland lineup to his St. Louis team.

At the end of the 1898 season, Robison transferred his best players to St. Louis, including ace pitcher Cy Young. The impact was immediate: whereas St. Louis, a last place team, climbed to fifth place in 1899, Cleveland, a moderately successful team, posted one of the worst records in baseball history, winning 20 games and losing 134.

Syndicate baseball was also hurting clubs in Baltimore and Louisville. By the National League's annual mid-winter meeting in 1899, it was obvious that something had to be done. National League owners dropped Cleveland, Baltimore and Louisville, as well as Washington, which also had financial problems. This left the National League with an eight-team circuit: four teams in the "west" (Chicago, St. Louis, Cincinnati, and Pittsburgh), and four teams in the "east" (Boston, Philadelphia, Brooklyn, and New York).

TOP TEN WORST RECORDS IN MAJOR LEAGUE BASEBALL

Season	Team	League	W	L	Pct.	GB
1899	Cleveland Spiders	National	20	134	.130	84
1890	Pittsburgh Pirates	National	23	113	.169	66½
1916	Philadelphia Athletics	American	36	117	.235	54½
1935	Boston Braves	National	38	115	.248	61½
1962	New York Mets	National	40	120	.250	60½
1904	Washington Senators	American	38	113	.252	55½
1919	Philadelphia Athletics	American	36	104	.257	52
1898	St. Louis Browns	National	39	111	.260	63½
2003	Detroit Tigers	American	43	119	.265	47
1952	Pittsburgh Pirates	National	42	112	.273	54½

Source: List of Worst Major League Baseball Season Records
(en.wikipedia.org)

The reaction was immediate. Alfred Spink called for yet another revival of the American Association.

Joining Spink were former American Association owners and several former National League owners, including some whose teams had just been dropped by the National League. Before the start of the 1900 season, the group proposed franchises in New York, St. Louis, Milwaukee, Detroit, Chicago, Baltimore, Philadelphia, and Washington. In order to calm the fears of minor league owners, the group announced that they would not raid minor league teams, but would focus their challenge exclusively on players from the National League.

As in the past, owners of National League teams responded to the challenge. Their first action was to go to court to bar the new league from using the name American Association. The National League had paid for the rights to the name in 1892 when eight teams from the National League merged with four teams from the American Association, forming the twelve-team circuit. Next, the National League proposed setting up its own major league, using the name the American Association. The intent was to have American Association teams play games in National League ballparks when the home team was on the road. Finally, National League owners called for the minor leagues to uphold the minor-major league agreement that established territorial and drafting rights for the major leagues.

The National League moves, however, didn't

dampen interest in establishing another major league. By February 1900, after renaming their enterprise the New American Base Ball Association, backers of the new league redoubled their efforts, promising franchises in Baltimore, Boston, Chicago, Philadelphia, Detroit, St. Louis, Milwaukee, and Providence. But when Chicago businessman James Gilmore, the main financial backer for the proposed league, failed to commit himself fully to the proposal, support for the New American Base Ball Association evaporated overnight.

Out of the Shadows

Throughout the struggle to revive the American Association, Johnson kept a low profile. When supporters of the plan asked Johnson to throw his lot in with them, Johnson declined the invitation. At the same time, Johnson didn't rush in to defend the National League either. Instead, Johnson proposed that the Western League expand into Chicago, a prosperous major league baseball market dominated by the National League. Johnson also proposed moving a franchise to Cleveland, a city recently abandoned by the National League after it slimmed down to an eight-team league.

Although there were some concerns about Johnson's proposed moves, National League owners were too preoccupied trying to stop the New American Base Ball Association from getting off the ground. Some owners, in fact, thought that Johnson's plans might keep the Association from invading those territories. Ultimately, the National League sanctioned Johnson's moves, but not without getting Johnson to agree upon several points.

First of all, Johnson agreed to honor the National Agreement, which meant he had to agree to the major league's right to draft minor league players. Johnson also agreed to pay for ballpark improvements to Cleveland's League Park, where Robison's Spiders had played. In addition, Johnson conceded two points to Jim Hart, Spalding's National League successor. He would have to give Hart two Western League draft picks. Johnson also agreed not to build a ballpark north of the stockyards on Chicago's south side.

Having conceded these points, Johnson moved the St. Paul club to Chicago and the Grand Rapids club to Cleveland. But he also did something else at the start of the 1900 season: Johnson renamed his organization the American League. Johnson now had teams in Chicago, Cleveland, Indianapolis, Detroit, Buffalo, Kansas City, Milwaukee, and Minneapolis. With his foot in the door of several National League cities, Johnson was ready to take the next step. Once again it came in response to the actions of National League owners.

Back row: Frank Navin, Benjamin Minor and Frank Farrell. Front row: Charles Comisky, Ban Johnson and Joseph Lannin.

AMERICAN LEAGUE PRESIDENT

Ban Johnson sitting for a photograph with franchise owners at their annual mid-winter meeting on Dec. 15, 1914. The former newspaper journalist and sports editor took a faltering minor league circuit, the Western League of Professional Baseball Clubs, and turned it into a nationally recognized major league on par with professional baseball's dominant National League. Posing with Johnson are team owners Frank Navin of Detroit, Washington's Benjamin Minor, New York's Frank Farrell, Chicago's Charles Comiskey, and Boston's Joseph Lannin.

After the New American Base Ball Association threat was clearly behind them, National League owners began to turn their attention to Johnson's growing empire. But the wealthy, all-powerful "League Magnates," as they referred to themselves, held different opinions about what to do. Some thought the best way to deal with Johnson was simply to ignore him. Others thought that a blatant snub would teach the upstart minor league president not to interfere with the National League.

In preparation for their annual mid-winter meeting in December of 1900, National League owners invited Johnson to New York to address the group. After Johnson arrived, team owners left him standing in the hallway outside the meeting room for several hours, then adjourned the meeting before asking him to join them inside. Furious, Johnson stormed out of the hotel and caught a train back to Chicago with only one thing in mind: to do everything within his power to undermine the National League.

Several months later, before the start of the 1901 season, Johnson made two announcements. First of all, he announced that the American League would be moving into four new markets: Baltimore, Washington, Philadelphia, and Boston (dropping Kansas City, Indianapolis, Minneapolis, and Buffalo). Secondly, Johnson announced that the American League would be national in scope and compete as a major league.

In order to stock teams with players, Johnson refused to acknowledge the minor-major league agreement, which gave the drafting rights of his American League players to the National League. At the same time, Johnson encouraged National League players who were reserved, but still without contract for the 1901 season, to join the American League. He did this the way every major league challenger did—with the promise of better pay. Once again, fate intervened.

With Open Arms

National League players were in the midst of rebelling against the restrictive practices of league owners, practices that included the enforcement of a $2,500 salary cap, the blacklisting of suspended players, and the use of the reserve clause that tied players to a team even after their contract had expired. Fed up with such practices, players formed the Players Protective Association, a players' union reminiscent of John Montgomery Ward's Brotherhood of Professional Base Ball Players that played a major role in the formation of the Players League in 1890.

Johnson made it known to players that not only would he recognize the Players Protective Association, but he would also adopt its uniform player contract (which the National League had soundly rejected) as the American League's model. And, of course, Johnson welcomed with open arms—and sizeable salary increases—any National League players who wished to sign with an American League team.

The ploy worked. Of the 182 players who signed up to play in the American League, almost two-thirds of them either had played for or were currently playing for a National League team. Some of the best known players who jumped leagues included Cy Young, Joe McGinnity, Nap Lajoie, Fielder Jones, Willie Keeler, Jimmy Collins, Chick Stahl, and Mike Donlin.

NAPOLEON ("NAP") LAJOIE signed with the National League's Philadelphia Phillies in 1896, but jumped to the American League in 1901, playing for Connie Mack's Philadelphia Athletics. A year later, Lajoie was traded to the Cleveland Bronchos after the Supreme Court of Pennsylvania upheld the reserve clause and the Phillies obtained an injunction barring Lajoie from playing baseball for any other team. Since the injunction was only enforceable in the state of Pennsylvania, Lajoie stayed home when the Bronchos (later renamed the "Naps" in honor of their star second baseman) played the Athletics in Philadelphia.

By the beginning of the 1901 season, Johnson had an eight-team league, seven of which were in either former or current National League cities. And, like the National League, Johnson's American League had four teams in the "west" (Cleveland, Detroit, Milwaukee, and Chicago), and four teams in the "east" (Baltimore, Washington, Philadelphia, and Boston).

But Johnson was still not through. In order to compete with the National League, Johnson needed an American League team in New York City, the nation's biggest baseball market and readily becoming the financial and cultural capital of the world.

Plans to place a team in New York hit a snag however. The problem was that the majority owner of the New York Giants, the autocratic Andrew Freedman, who bought the debt-ridden Giants in 1895, had political ties to corrupt officials at City Hall. Whenever Johnson proposed to buy or lease a piece of property for the purpose of building a ballpark, city officials either condemned the property, leased it to someone else, or built a trolley line through it.

For a year and a half, Freedman, one of the National League's most cantankerous owners, thwarted Johnson's efforts to enter the New York market, the most prestigious—and potentially the most lucrative—market in all of major league baseball.

With my team I am an absolute czar.
John McGraw

CHAPTER THREE

Double-crossed

JOHNSON WOULD HAVE stayed thwarted had not Andrew Freedman made an error in judgment. Freedman had teamed up with John Brush, who besides owning the National League's Cincinnati team also had a stake in Freedman's Giants. At the National League's annual mid-winter meeting in 1901, Freedman and Brush proposed that the eight-team league consolidate into a single corporation. Of the other six owners, only Arthur Soden of Boston and Frank Robison of St. Louis agreed to support Freedman and Brush's proposal.

According to the plan, the National League would operate as a single corporation instead of a loosely knit federation of independent ball clubs. The league would rename itself the National Baseball Trust and would elect a five-member Board of Regents to govern it. The board would hire a president, assign all team managers, and license players (who could be moved from team to team whenever the Board of Regents deemed it necessary in order to maintain equality among the league's teams). This was syndicate baseball at its worst.

The plan was flawed from the beginning, however, because teams did not have an equal share in the corporation. Owners received a percentage of stock in the trust based upon their size and their ability to generate gate receipts. Naturally, clubs that received the greatest percentage of stock (New York 30%, Cincinnati 12%, St. Louis 12%, and Boston 12%) were delighted and supported the plan. Clubs that received a lesser percentage (Chicago 10%, Philadelphia 10%, Pittsburgh 8%, and Brooklyn 6%) were less enthusiastic and opposed the plan.

Unable to break the 4-4 split on the proposal, owners turned their attention to the re-election of league president Nick Young. Young was a former player and league umpire, and before serving as president had been the league's secretary-treasurer. Here again, the owners split 4-4, with New York's Freedman leading one faction in favor of Young and Chicago's Jim Hart leading another group against Young.

In order to break the stalemate, Hart nominated Al Spalding for league president. Spalding was Hart's predecessor in Chicago. He had a stellar baseball career. He had pitched for both Boston and Chicago, was co-owner of the National League's Chicago team, and was a past National League president. Even in his *ex officio* capacity, Spalding still called many of the shots when it came to league policy, though his influence was waning as his attention was diverted more and more to his thriving sporting goods empire.

Spalding accepted the nomination in order to block Freedman and Brush's proposal. Not only did the four syndicate backers—Freedman, Brush, Soden, and Robison—not support Spalding's nomination, they stormed out of the meeting leaving the remaining owners without a quorum necessary to vote on the nomination. But the remaining owners, who were whole-heartedly against the trust idea, voted anyway and Spalding was named league president.

That night Spalding marched over to Nick Young's hotel room to collect the league's records. While Spalding and Young argued in the hallway, Spalding's porter slipped into the room, scooped up the records, and hustled them back to Spalding's quarters.

The next morning Spalding called a meeting of the league's owners. Naturally, only Spalding's allies showed up. When he saw Fred Knowles, the secretary-treasurer of the New York Giants, spying on the meeting from the doorway, Spalding declared a quorum and the group voted down Freedman and Brush's baseball trust idea. Then before Freedman and Brush could get a court order to stop him, Spalding packed up the league's records and headed back to Chicago.

Spalding, however, had no interest in being league president. His sporting goods empire was booming and he wanted nothing more than to abandon league politics and concentrate exclusively on his business interests. To resolve the conflict, Spalding, ever the shrewd businessman, made it known to league owners that he would step down as the league's president, but only if Freedman sold his interest in the Giants, which Freedman had notoriously mismanaged ever since he bought controlling interest in the club.

With the 1902 season around the corner, and Johnson's American League raiding National League teams, a deal was struck. Freedman sold his interest in the Giants to Brush. Brush, in turn, sold his interest in the Reds to Cincinnati businessman Garry Herrmann (part of a group of Cincinnati businessmen headed by the city's political boss George Cox). Then, Brush, Soden and Hart formed an executive committee to run the league until they could elect a league president.

With the syndicate plan abandoned and the mischievous Freedman on his way out of the league, Spalding returned to Chicago to oversee his business interests. This was just the break Johnson was waiting for, except while owners of the National League were fighting over the syndicate plan, Johnson was dealing with his own headache — John Joseph ("Muggsy") McGraw.

Little Napoleon

As president of the Western League, Johnson had his supporters. Besides Charles Comiskey and Connie Mack, Johnson had the financial backing of Charles Somers and John Kilfoyle of Cleveland and Ben Shibe of Philadelphia. He also had the support of several key National League players, including pitching ace Clark Griffith and Baltimore Orioles' third baseman John McGraw.

McGraw, one of the league's most aggressive players, started his major league baseball career in Baltimore in 1891 at the age of eighteen. Within three years, McGraw was playing third base and batting .340. Along with teammate ("Wee") Willie Keeler, he was generally considered one of the league's best hitters, a master of fouling off pitches until he had either slashed a base hit or secured a base on balls.

CORNELIUS MCGILLICUDDY also known as Connie Mack, managed the American League's Philadelphia Athletics for 50 seasons before retiring in 1950 at the age of 87. During his tenure with the Athletics, Mack won nine American League pennants and five World Series championships. Along with Charles Comiskey, Mack was a founding member of the American League and staunch supporter of Ban Johnson's idea that in

 order to attract a large paying audience, professional baseball had to be free from drinking, gambling, and rowdy behavior. To this extent, Mack drew up and enforced the following nine principles of player conduct:

→ *I will always play the game to the best of my ability.*

→ *I will always play to win, but if I lose, I will not look for an excuse to detract from my opponent's victory.*

→ *I will never take an unfair advantage in order to win.*

→ *I will always abide by the rules of the game, on the diamond as well as in my daily life.*

→ *I will always conduct myself as a true sportsman, on and off the playing field.*

→ *I will always strive for the good of the entire team rather than for my own glory.*

→ *I will never gloat in victory or pity myself in defeat.*

→ *I will do my utmost to keep myself clean: physically, mentally, and morally.*

→ *I will always judge a teammate or an opponent as an individual and never on the basis or race or religion.*

Source: The Bill James Guide to Baseball Managers.

More than his playing ability, however, the hot-tempered, sharp-tongued McGraw—often called "Little Napoleon"—brought to the team a combative, warlike spirit. Under the influence of McGraw, the "Old Orioles" of the 1890s were an unruly, aggressive, even mean-spirited team. Players saw nothing wrong with spiking opposing players, shoving umpires, or jumping into the stands to pummel a noisy spectator. The Orioles were rowdy, loud, and confrontational. At the same time, they were disciplined and alert, which is why they dominated their league.

They were one of the leading teams in the 1890s—until 1899. That year Harry von der Horst, who was the majority owner of the Orioles, and Gus Abell, who owned the Brooklyn Bridegrooms, bought equal shares of each other's team, and agreed to move Baltimore's best players to Brooklyn, an emerging baseball market.

However, McGraw and teammate Wilbert Robinson, two of the best players on the Baltimore team, stayed behind. Baltimore was their home. Fans adored them. Besides, they owned a profitable business, the Diamond Cafe, which had become a favorite haunt for Baltimore's sporting crowd.

But the Baltimore assignment, with McGraw as the team's player-manager and Robinson his right-hand man, lasted only a year. At the end of the 1899 season, the twelve-team National League, feeling the negative effects of syndicate baseball, slimmed down to an eight-team league, and Baltimore, Cleveland, Louisville, and Washington were dropped.

IN 1890, THE BROOKLYN BRIDE-GROOMS left the American Association and joined the National League. The name "bride-grooms" referred to the fact that several Brooklyn players had recently gotten married. Nine years later, in 1899, the club changed its name to the BROOKLYN SUPERBAS (named after part-owner Ned Hanlon's acting company) when the National League's Baltimore Orioles purchased half-interest in the Bridegrooms, moving the heart of the "Old Orioles" to Brooklyn. After their home field burned to the ground in 1911, the Superbas moved to nearby Eastern Park. Since the park was wedged between several trolley car lines, the press called the team the BROOKLYN TROLLEY DODGERS, a reference to fans who had to dodge the trolley lines crisscrossing Brooklyn at the time. The name was shortened to BROOKLYN DODGERS in 1913 when the team moved to Ebbets Field. In 1914, the club's owners dropped Brooklyn Dodgers and began calling the team the BROOKLYN ROBINS in honor of their new manager Wilbert ("Uncle Robbie") Robinson. They remained the Robins for the next eighteen years, until Robinson retired in

1931 and the team reverted back to the Dodgers moniker. But in 1958 the team's named changed again—to the Los Angeles Dodgers—*after club owners moved the franchise from New York to southern California.*

In order to stay in organized baseball, McGraw and Robinson quickly jumped on the bandwagon led by Alfred Spink to revive the old American Association, even assembling a group of investors to sponsor a Baltimore team. When attempts to revive the American Association collapsed, McGraw and Robinson found themselves in an awkward position: they were still under contract to the National League due to their reserve status. Instead of releasing them from their contract, National League officials decided to banish them to the ends of the baseball world: they were traded to St. Louis. But they didn't go easily.

McGraw and Robinson refused to show up for spring training. They were angry about having to move so far away from their thriving business, which made them more money than their league salaries. McGraw also held out for another reason: he wanted a better deal. After all, he was considered one of the best players of the era.

Frank Robison, who held controlling interest in the St. Louis Cardinals (formerly the Perfectos), must have had the same opinion. Robison offered the feisty third baseman $5,000 in salary, $3,500 of McGraw's purchase price, and an additional $1,000 signing bonus. All totaled, McGraw would reap $9,500, the largest sum a ballplayer had ever been paid.

But McGraw wanted something else, something more valuable. He refused to play until the National League waived the reserve clause for both him and teammate Wilbert Robinson. When league officials agreed, McGraw and Robinson boarded a train and headed to St. Louis.

The Only Rules He Knew

McGraw, however, was already looking ahead. While playing for the Cardinals during the 1900 season, McGraw contacted Ban Johnson of the American League. In order to move back to Baltimore, and to avenge the National League for exiling him to St. Louis, McGraw coaxed Johnson into sponsoring an American League team in Baltimore for the 1901 season. At the end of the 1900 season, with their reserve clause waived, McGraw and Robinson hopped a train to Baltimore, dumping their Cardinals' uniforms into the Mississippi River as they headed north.

From the beginning, however, McGraw proved to be more than Johnson had bargained for. Schooled in the Old Orioles way of doing things, McGraw coached the team to be as verbally abusive and phys-ically aggressive as his old team. As the team's manager, McGraw specialized in the mistreatment of umpires, an activity to which he had no equal.

McGraw's abuse of umpires, however, rubbed Johnson the wrong way. When Johnson organized the American League, he emphasized the need for club managers to respect and support league umpires, who were hired by the league and not by individual clubs. Johnson was quite prepared to fine or suspend anyone, player or manager, who wouldn't abide by this rule.

McGraw didn't give a hoot about Johnson's rules. The only rules McGraw knew were the ones that helped him win, and that meant he did whatever he had to on the field to come out on top. As such, it didn't take long before the fiery, umpire-baiting McGraw locked horns with the stern, dictatorial Johnson.

Throughout the 1901 season, McGraw repeatedly antagonized American League umpires, often incur-ring Johnson's wrath. As a result, Johnson just as often fined or suspended McGraw for his abusive behavior. As the tension grew between the two men, McGraw began to wonder if Johnson would take him to New York when the American League moved into the National League's most prized territory.

Umpires Ernie Quigley, Tom Connolly, Hank O'Day, and Bill Dinneen—1916 World Series.

WITH THE PROFESSIONALISM *of base-ball in the 1880s, umpiring became an official part of the game. National League president William Hulbert assembled the first umpire staff, identifying a group of twenty men from which teams could tap. From the start, however, umpiring was not only difficult, it was dangerous. Umpires were routinely spiked, kicked, cursed, and spat upon by players and managers. Fans took out their frustration on umpires, too, so much so that umpires often needed a police escort on and off the field. It was only with the peace agreement of 1903, between the National League and the American League, that stability—as well as increased pay and stature—was brought to the profession.*

The 1902 season began ominously, with McGraw being ejected from the season opener in Boston. Umpire Tom Connolly, aware of McGraw's umpire-baiting tactics, ejected McGraw from the game after a few innings of abuse. Connolly was not the only American League umpire who dealt harshly with the antagonistic McGraw.

In April, again in a game against Boston, umpire Jack Sheridan stood by and watched as Boston's starting pitcher hit McGraw with five different pitches. But Sheridan refused to give McGraw a base on balls in each case, saying McGraw purposely stood in the way of the pitch to draw a walk. After the fifth episode, which occurred in the ninth inning, McGraw sat down in the batter's box and refused to move until he was physically removed from the game. When Johnson learned of McGraw's insolence, he was furious and suspended the grandstanding McGraw for five games.

During his suspension, McGraw took a trip to New York, to visit Andrew Freedman, the outgoing owner of the New York Giants. McGraw, always looking out for his own interests, was forging his own plans to make it to New York. After serving the five-game suspension, McGraw returned to the Orioles, but his demeanor had not been tamed. In fact, McGraw seemed to play with a vengeance, going out of his way to antagonize American League umpires.

In a game in late June, McGraw so irritated Tom Connolly that his old nemesis threw him out of the game in the eighth inning. Again, McGraw refused to leave the field. This time, however, Connolly called the game and the Orioles forfeited to Boston.

When Johnson found out about the incident, he was furious. He suspended McGraw indefinitely, proclaiming to the press that he would not tolerate such rowdy behavior from any player. McGraw went on his own tirade against Johnson, characterizing him as a dictator who treated players like cattle, always cracking a whip over them. McGraw ended his tongue-lashing of Johnson with the final admonition that ultimately a man must look out for himself.

And look out for himself—he did.

The Consummate Dealmaker

Within days, McGraw made a stunning announcement: he would manage the New York Giants for a whopping $11,000 a year. McGraw, ever the self-promoter, had negotiated a four-year contract with outgoing Giants' owner Andrew Freedman with the tacit approval of incoming majority owner John Brush.

In order to close the deal, McGraw had to get out of his Baltimore contract. To do this, McGraw asked the Orioles' management for the immediate payment of a $7,000 loan that McGraw had made to the organization earlier in the season to cover team expenses. When the Orioles couldn't come up with the cash, McGraw offered to waive the debt if the team would release him from his contract. They did, and McGraw was free to leave, but before leaving McGraw did something else to further infuriate Johnson.

McGraw transferred a majority of Baltimore stock to Freedman, giving the National League owner a controlling interest in the American League team. McGraw did this secretly with the help of John ("Sonny") Mahon, a rising figure in Baltimore's political machinery. McGraw and Mahon cobbled together 201 of the 400 shares of the Baltimore club, combining the shares owned by McGraw, Mahon, and teammates Joe Kelly (Mahon's son-in-law), and Wilbert Robinson (who exchanged his shares in the Orioles for McGraw's shares in the Diamond Cafe).

To complete the deal, Mahon transferred the shares to attorney Joseph France, who was acting as trustee for New York Giants' owner Andrew Freedman. Once the shares were transferred, Freedman released fourteen of Baltimore's players, signing four of the best players to his National League team in New York, including first baseman Dan McGann, catcher Roger Bresnahan, and pitchers Joe McGinnity and Jack Cronin.

When he learned of the plan in late July after the Orioles failed to field a team against St. Louis, Johnson was beside himself. But he remained calm and took immediate action. First of all, he revoked the Baltimore team's franchise, taking over the club himself, filling its roster with second-rate players from other American League teams. At the same time, Johnson redoubled his efforts to place an American League team in New York City.

BALTIMORE ARRIVED on the professional baseball scene early, becoming a charter member of the American Association in 1882. From the start, it was a powerful and innovative team, joining the National League ten years later when the American Association folded. In their day, however, the "Old Orioles" were the team to beat as they featured some of the best baseball talent of the era, including Wilbert Robinson, John McGraw, Hughie Jennings, and Willie Keeler. They appeared in all four Temple Cup matches (1894-1897), a best-of-seven, post-season championship series sponsored by the National League, winning two of the four.

Managed by Ned Hanlon, an intelligent, innovative manager, the Orioles perfected the game of "inside baseball," preferring "the hit-and-run" to "the long ball." But that was to be expected in the "dead ball" era, when baseballs were soft and mushy. Despite their success throughout the late 1890s, the Orioles were dropped from the National League in 1899, when the National League slimmed down from twelve to eight franchises.

When Hanlon moved to Brooklyn to manage the Bridegrooms, the Orioles struggled, as Hanlon took the core of the Orioles with him. Only Robinson and McGraw stayed behind, supporting an effort to revive the American Association. When that effort failed, Robinson and McGraw signed with the National League's St. Louis franchise, bringing to a close the Old Orioles' era.

Keep your eye clear and hit 'em where they ain't.
Willie Keeler

CHAPTER FOUR

New York at Last

DESPITE BEING HOODWINKED by the Giants, Ban Johnson knew that his fortunes in New York would soon be changing. What gave Johnson hope was the fact that Andrew Freedman was on his way out as the club's principal owner, thanks to Spalding who, in the wake of the National Baseball Trust fiasco, forced Freedman to sell his interests in the Giants' franchise. The change came in September of 1902 when Freedman officially resigned, naming John Brush, Johnson's nemesis from his newspaper days in Ohio, the team's new majority owner and president.

Although Brush was as autocratic as Freedman, Brush lacked something that Freedman enjoyed—connections to New York City's corrupt officials. Even if Freedman had not stepped down, Johnson would still have had a good chance of moving Baltimore's American League franchise to New York. In the city's November elections, a slate of reform-minded candidates headed by major-elect Seth Low ousted many former officials.

Despite the change in political winds, Johnson's optimism was a combination of changing circumstances and his own will to succeed. Given the continuing presence of Brush and McGraw, and Freedman who still exerted influence over New York City politics and National League decisions, Johnson decided that the best way to gain a foothold in the New York baseball market was to beat the National League at its own game. So Johnson went in search of men who had their own connections to New York City officials, finding them in two underworld characters: Frank Farrell and William ("Big Bill") Devery.

FOR MUCH OF THE LATE 1880s and early 1900s, the seat of power in New York City resided in Tammany Hall, a reference to the Tammany Society of New York City, founded in 1786 as a fraternal organization whose activities were primarily social. Over time the activities of the Tammany Society became overtly political and aligned with the city's corrupt Democratic Party machinery. For eight decades, officials directed the flow of money, patronage, and votes until 1932 when Mayor James Walker was forced from

office. This, along with the effects of the Great
Depression and the election of President Roo-
sevelt, severely diminished the power and influence
of Tammany Hall.

Frank Farrell, an ex-bartender, was known as New York's "Pool Room King" for his controlling interest in dozens of pool halls, or "gambling dens," scattered throughout Lower Manhattan. Saloons and racehorses were among his other holdings. In other words, Farrell was a man of means and influence.

Bill Devery, a former bartender and prizefighter, was also a man with money and influence. Early in his career his money came from graft and corruption while working for the New York Police Department. Later, it came from shrewd real estate investments, which he oversaw from his estate in Far Rockaway, Queens. What the two men had in common, and what Johnson needed most, were ties to New York City's political machinery.

With the 1903 season fast approaching, Farrell and Devery bought the Baltimore franchise from Johnson for $18,000 on the condition that they relocate the club to Manhattan. They did, leasing a piece of property in the Washington Heights section of upper Manhattan. But their plans to build a ballpark did not proceed without some resistance.

Brush, who was now in full control of the Giants, did everything he could to stop Johnson from invading New York, especially Manhattan where the Giants played. With Freedman's help, Brush obtained options on any vacant lot in Manhattan he thought the American League could use to build a ballpark. When he got to 155th Street, Brush stopped, thinking he was safe as the property in upper Manhattan was nothing but a pile of rocks, unsuitable for a ballpark.

He was wrong.

Hilltoppers

Farrell and Devery leased a piece of property owned by the New York Institute for the Blind between 165th and 168th Streets and Fort Washington Avenue and Broadway. Caught off guard, Brush petitioned the Washington Heights District Governing Board to stop construction on the grounds that a ballpark would attract "undesirables" to the neighborhood. But the five-member board voted on a narrow margin of 3-2 to support Farrell and Devery and construction on a new ballpark began immediately.

The first job was by far the most difficult: they had to level a huge mountain of rock that rose from the middle of the property, which was just under 10 acres. After several days of blasting, and several more days of rough-grading the property, construction finally began.

The ballpark, also known as Hilltop Park, featured a single-deck grandstand that wrapped around home plate, and two long bleacher sections that stretched the length of the foul lines on either side of the grandstand. In all, the grandstand and bleachers held close to 16,000 fans, with room for hundreds more who could stand just outside the first and third base foul lines or several men deep behind the outfielders.

Farrell and Devery named former coal-mining executive Joseph Gordon the team's president. It was a deal they worked out with Johnson, who wanted a more acceptable face to the American League franchise than Farrell and Devery's.

It was Gordon who suggested the team's name—the Highlanders—in part because the ballpark perched on one of the highest spots in Washington Heights, but also because a crack British regiment by the same name was touring America at the time and their commander was also named Gordon.

But the British-sounding name didn't go over very well with local fans, many of whom were Irish Catholics and disliked the British. So, from the beginning, the Highlanders went by various names: Hilltoppers, Burglars, Porch Climbers, New Yorkers, Americans, and, the New York press's favorite, Yanks or Yankees.

Hilltop opened its doors on April 30, 1903, even though part of the outfield was roped off to keep

Batting practice before a game in 1911 at American League Park, also known as Hilltop Park.

players from stumbling into a small gully that workers had not had time to fill. A capacity crowd flowed through the gates that day, each fan receiving a small American flag, thanks to American League president Ban Johnson, who was on hand for the opening-day ceremonies. Farrell and Devery were there as well, as were many of their political cronies.

After Old Glory was hoisted to the top of the flagpole, and the 69th Regiment Band played a medley of patriotic songs—including "Hail, Columbia," "Columbia, Gem of the Ocean" and "Yankee Doodle"—the Highlanders took the field in their white uniforms and white flannel caps with black lacing. The Highlanders didn't disappoint the overflow crowd either, beating the Washington Senators 6-2.

Under the leadership of player-manager Clark Griffith, a former National League star and one of Ban Johnson's earliest supporters, the Highlanders took fourth place in their first season behind the pitching of ("Happy") Jack Chesbro, who had his best season that year, winning 41 games, still an American League record. The other star was Willie Keeler, a former teammate of John McGraw and Wilbert Robinson. Unlike McGraw and Robinson, however, Keeler went to Brooklyn with Orioles' manager Ned Hanlon, but jumped leagues when Johnson formed the American League.

The 1903 season was important not only because it was the inaugural year for the Highlanders, it was also the year in which National League owners finally agreed to sit down with Johnson and work out an agreement between the two leagues. The vote to do so came at the end of the season, during the National League's annual mid-winter meeting in New York. Every National League owner, except one, voted to make peace with Johnson. The one dissenting vote was John Brush, whose clashes with the American League president went back to Johnson's days as sports editor of the *Cincinnati Commercial-Gazette*.

The signed accord, known as the National Agreement of 1903, forced the two leagues to recognize each other as separate and equal organizations. It also established a three-man governing board made up of the two league presidents and one elected board chairman. As American League president, Johnson sat on the board, and, by force of his personality, influenced its decisions until a single Commissioner of Baseball replaced the board in 1920.

High Hopes

The Highlanders' second season was even better than the first. At the end of the 154-game season, the Highlanders found themselves going into the final weekend of play a game behind the Boston Americans. They had two more games to play: a doubleheader at Hilltop against the first-place Americans. To win the league's pennant, the Highlanders had to win both games.

Hilltop was packed with a standing-room-only crowd of over twenty-eight thousand. There were so many fans that ropes were placed in the outfield in order to admit as many fans as possible.

The first game of the double-header was billed as a pitcher's duel, between Boston's Bill Dinneen and New York's Jack Chesbro, the team's best hurler. The billing was correct: it was a low-scoring game that went into the ninth inning tied at two apiece.

In the top of the ninth, Boston's Lou Criger beat out an infield single; then took second on a sacrifice by Dinneen. When Boston's next batter hit into a force out, Criger took third. With Freddie Parent, Boston's shortstop, at bat, and Criger dancing off third ninety feet away, Chesbro hunkered down. It took less than half a dozen pitches to get the count to two balls and two strikes. Now, Chesbro only needed one more strike to end Boston's threat. Chesbro reeled back and unleashed his signature pitch—a spitball.

Much to the horror of the Highlanders' fans, Chesbro's pitch sailed over the head of catcher Red Kleinow and rolled some ninety feet to the backstop. Criger scored easily. When the Highlanders failed to score in the bottom of the ninth, the game was over, and so was their most promising season. Although they won the second game 1-0, a dispirited Highlander team took second place. It would be the closest they'd get to capturing the pennant at Hilltop.

Even if the Highlanders had won the double-header at Hilltop and clinched the American League pennant, they would not have played a championship series against the National League pennant winner. The reason was simple: there wasn't one that year because John McGraw, supported by New York Giants' owner John Brush, refused to play against the winner of what McGraw derisively considered a minor league.

Even though the leagues had signed a peace accord the year before, and the National League's Pittsburgh Pirates had played the American League's Boston Pilgrims for the 1903 championship title (and lost five games to three), the headstrong McGraw argued that there was nothing in the National League's constitution to force him to play in a post-season championship series. Post-season competition would have to wait one more year, until 1905, after major league's three-man governing board set down the rules for such play.

Prince Hal

During their third season, the Highlanders acquired another headline name: Hal Chase, known as "Prince Hal" or "The Magician." Chase was an enormously gifted first baseman who was brought from the Pacific Coast League. Considered by many one of the finest fielding first basemen in history, Chase was agile, graceful, and quick-witted, and for a moment the Highlanders looked like there was nowhere to go but up.

But for all his ability, Chase was arrogant and unprincipled, and from the start many of his teammates suspected him of throwing games. By 1907, instead of a first-rate team, the Highlanders were at best mediocre, which meant the franchise was a financial liability.

During the season, Farrell and Devery demoted Gordon to vice-president and began running the day-to-day operations themselves (firing Gordon at the end of the season). The constant meddling in the team's affairs irked manager Clark Griffith, but he continued to manage as best he could, opening the 1908 season with a winning record. But when the Highlanders went into a tailspin during the month of June, Farrell and Devery had had enough and fired Griffith, replacing him with the team's shortstop, Norman ("Kid") Elberfeld. But Elberfeld couldn't turn the team around and the Highlanders finished the 1908 season at the bottom, this time with a 51-103 record, their worst yet.

To manage the team next, Farrell and Devery turned to George Stallings, a former ballplayer who had successfully managed teams in Philadelphia and Detroit. With Stallings at the helm, the Highlanders started to play better ball, and by the middle of the 1910 season were on their way to a second-place finish behind Connie Mack's Philadelphia Athletics. Then misfortune struck.

Stallings, who had his own suspicions about Chase, accused the flamboyant first baseman of throwing games. Incensed by the accusations, Chase complained directly to league president Ban Johnson. When Johnson failed to back Stallings, Chase went to Farrell and Devery and told the owners that if they didn't fire Stallings he would quit.

When Farrell and Devery sided with their star player, Stallings packed his bags. The Highlanders still finished in second place, but a distant fifteen games behind Philadelphia. Even so, this should have lifted team spirits, but it didn't. When Farrell and Devery announced that Chase would manage the team in 1911, players rebelled, as they already knew Chase to be arrogant and self-serving.

HAROLD ("HAL") CHASE *was one of the best fielding first basemen of his era. Chase (left, shaking hands with New York Giants' manager John McGraw), began his career with the Pacific Coast League, and played major league baseball for four teams over a fifteen-year career. Despite his stellar play as a defensive first baseman and a superb hitter, Chase was plagued with accusations of cheating throughout his career. The accusations finally came to a head at the end of the 1918 season, a season that Chase, playing for Cincinnati, sat out because of a suspension for allegedly paying a teammate $50 to throw a game. When*

National League president John Heydler received an envelope from an anonymous source containing a copy of a check for $500 that Chase had received from a gambler to throw a different game during the 1918 season, Chase's career was effectively over. He was released from the Giants who had signed him in 1919, and although he was never officially banned from the sport he never played in the major leagues again.

Chase's tenure at the helm, however, was short-lived. After a disappointing season in which the Highlanders finished in sixth place, 25½ games out of first place, Farrell and Devery fired Chase, released him from his contract, and brought in cigar-smoking Harry Wolverton. Wolverton promptly announced that the Highlanders would go to the top in one season. Instead, they went straight to the bottom, finishing 55 games out of first place. At season's end, Farrell and Devery gave Wolverton the boot.

It was the end of the 1912 season. Farrell and Devery had gone through five managers in ten seasons, and the Highlanders, a lousy team, were hemorrhaging money. And, yet, as their ten-year lease at Hilltop was drawing to a close, Farrell and Devery still looked toward the future, hoping to build a new ballpark for the franchise.

A Favor Returned

Several locations stood out. There was a large parcel of land available on Broadway in the Bronx. In Brooklyn, Washington Park was available. But each location had its drawbacks: for the Bronx property, it was securing enough financial backing to build a new ballpark; for Washington Park, it was asking their fan base, mostly from upper Manhattan, to travel to Brooklyn for the club's home games.

At the same time Farrell and Devery were discussing the Highlanders' future after Hilltop, the aging and wheelchair-bound John Brush, the majority owner of the New York Giants, died. The event prompted Farrell and Devery to consider a third option: leasing the Polo Grounds for the Highlanders' home games. It was a logical choice as the Polo Grounds required little upfront money to lease and its proximity to Hilltop would not inconvenience its fan base.

So, in the fall of 1912, Farrell and Devery approached Harry Hempstead, Brush's son-in-law and the Giants' newly appointed club president, to discuss the prospect of leasing the Giants' home field. They did so not only because of Brush's death, but also because the Giants owed them a favor, or so they thought.

The favor occurred the prior year when Farrell

and Devery invited the Giants to play the first half of the 1911 season at Hilltop Park after a fire destroyed the Polo Grounds at the start of the season. Of course, Farrell and Devery hoped Hempstead would remember the act of kindness, which *The New York Times* called "the brightest spot in local baseball competition."

Hempstead did, and the Highlanders began the 1913 season as co-tenants of the Giants at the Polo Grounds. The beginning of the season was memorable for another reason: the Highlanders formally made the name change to the Yankees, which sportswriters had been using on and off for several years as it was less cumbersome than the eleven-character Highlanders' name.

Not only did the Highlanders begin the 1913 season with a new name and a new home field, they also began with a new manager by the name of Frank Chance, a tough ballplayer-turned-manager who was known in major league baseball for his success managing the National League's Chicago Cubs. In his eight-year stint as manager, Chance led the Cubs to four National League pennants and two World Series championships.

But as tough as he was, the Yankees finished in seventh place, and were headed in the same direction by the end of the 1914 season. With seventeen games left in the season, Farrell and Devery fired Chance and replaced him with their 23-year-old shortstop, Roger Peckinpaugh, the team's best player.

But the Yankees weren't the only ones hurting. Farrell and Devery had made several poor investments and were broke. By the end of the 1914 season, they made it known in New York baseball circles the Yankees were for sale.

THE POLO GROUNDS gets its name from the original use of a parcel of land just north of Central Park between 5th and 6th Avenues and 110th Street. It was the site of amateur polo matches during most of the 1870s.

A decade later, professional baseball took over the site, hosting two major league teams. The National League's New York Giants played in the southeast corner, while the American Association's New York Metropolitans played in the southwest corner. When the Giants were evicted from the site in 1889, the team moved to Manhattan Field, built in Coogan's Hollow between 155th and 157th Streets.

Despite the new location, the Giants continued using the old name—the Polo Grounds. Again, two major league teams dominated the site: a team representing the Players League (also called the Giants) played in Brotherhood Park, just north of where the National League's New York Giants played.

When the Players League folded at the end of the 1890 season, the National League Giants moved into Brotherhood Park, renaming the ballpark the Polo Grounds. Brotherhood Park featured a two-story wood and steel grandstand that wrapped around home plate in the shape of a horseshoe, which meant that there were very short distances to the left and right field walls and an unusually deep center field.

The third reincarnation of the Polo Grounds stood for almost twenty years, until a fire of unknown origin swept through the ballpark on Friday, April 14, 1911, consuming most of the wooden grandstand. While the Polo Grounds were being rebuilt as a steel-and-concrete structure, the Giants played their home games at Hilltop Park, invited to do so by the owners of the American League's Hilltop Highlanders. The Polo Grounds reopened on June 28, 1911, after two-and-a-half months of construction, becoming the ninth steel-and-concrete stadium in the major leagues.

Two years later, grateful to the Highlanders for allowing the Giants to play their home games at Hilltop Park, the Giants leased the newly renovated Polo Grounds to the Highlanders (now called the Yankees) after the Highlanders' lease on Hilltop Park expired at the end of the 1912 season.

When the Yankees moved to their new stadium at the end of the 1922 season, the Giants *continued to play their home games at the Polo Grounds, until the team's owners decided to move the organization to the west coast at the end of the 1957 season, where they became the San Francisco Giants. But that would not be the last major league baseball game played at the Polo Grounds before it was demolished in 1964.*

New York City's newest franchise, the New York Mets, played their first two seasons (1962-1963) at the Polo Grounds while their home ballpark—Shea Stadium—was being built in Queens.

*A good manager has his cards dealt to him
and he must play them.*

Miller Huggins

CHAPTER FIVE

Looking for a Plaything

BY THE SECOND decade of the twentieth century, professional baseball was unmistakably America's number one sport, its "national pastime." In New York, the team to watch was John McGraw's New York Giants. McGraw had taken a hapless, ill-starred team and turned it into a first-rate contender. Fans flocked to the Polo Grounds in upper Manhattan to watch the Giants, who, by season's end, were more likely than not to be in the hunt for the National League pennant.

Among the fans that crowded into the Polo Grounds to watch the Giants play was the impeccably dressed Col. Jacob ("Jake") Ruppert. Heir to his immigrant father's brewing business, Ruppert was a bachelor who lived in a lavish fifteen-room mansion on Fifth Avenue, cared for by his butler, maid, cook, laundress, and personal valet. Ruppert, a member of the 7th Regiment of the New York National Guard, obtained the honorary colonelship with his appointment to the staff of Governor David Hill. With Tammany Hall backing, Ruppert was elected to Congress in 1898, representing New York's Fifteenth Congressional District. He served four consecutive terms before stepping down to run his father's burgeoning brewing business.

Ruppert lived a privileged life, his great wealth allowing him many luxuries. He owned a country estate, dubbed "Eagle's Rest," in Garrison, New York, across the Hudson River from the U.S. Military Academy at West Point. He kept a yacht, christened "The Albatross." He raised champion St. Bernards that he exhibited at the Westminster Kennel Club. He owned a stable of racehorses, a troop of monkeys, a cabinet

Col. Jake Ruppert (seated, front right) and T. L. ("Cap") Huston (seated, back left) join New York City Mayor John Purroy Mitchell (seated, front left) at a New York Yankees' home game at the Polo Grounds at the start of the 1914 season. Ruppert and Huston would purchase the franchise the following year.

full of rare books, and a shelf of jade and porcelain figurines. In short, Jake Ruppert was a well-groomed, stylish bachelor who liked to collect things, and now he had his eye on a major league baseball team—the National League's New York Giants.

After Brush died unexpectedly in 1912, Ruppert approached McGraw to see if Brush's heirs would sell the team, but the family was still in mourning over the loss of its patriarch and declined the offer. When Ruppert inquired again at the end of the 1914 season, after turning down a chance to buy the National League's Chicago Cubs, McGraw introduced Ruppert to another wealthy baseball enthusiast, his close friend Tillinghast L'Hommedieu ("Cap") Huston.

Huston was the opposite of Ruppert. He had a modest upbringing in Ohio here he studied to be an engineer. When the Spanish-American War broke out, Huston went to Cuba as a captain in the Second Volunteer Engineer Corps. After the war, Huston stayed in Cuba, helping to rebuild Havana and other port cities, and in the process amassed a fortune. He was a heavyset man with an outgoing personality. He loved to drink and have a good time. And, unlike the fastidiously dressed Ruppert, Huston's taste in clothes was limited to the same rumpled suit and derby he wore almost every day. The only things Ruppert and Huston had in common were money and a growing interest in major league baseball.

After McGraw, who had met Huston on a trip to Cuba, introduced the two men, he pointed them in the direction of Farrell and Devery, who were looking for a buyer for their faltering American League team. The foursome met in December of 1914 and within weeks struck a deal. On January 11, 1915, Ruppert and Huston announced that they had just bought the New York Yankees for $460,000 in cash.

Although the Yankees were a far cry from the mighty Giants, that didn't seem to bother Ruppert and Huston who set out immediately to strengthen their newly-acquired team. The first order of business was to hire a manager. They settled on ("Wild") Bill Donovan, a former first-rate pitcher for the Detroit Tigers and a successful minor league manager in the International League. Then, the two owners turned their attention to buying the best players they could get. Their first purchases included ace pitcher Bob Shawkey from the Philadelphia Athletics and first baseman Wally Pipp from the Detroit Tigers.

The acquisition of Pipp signaled a new direction for the team. Pipp was a power hitter who led the league in home runs two years in a row with totals of twelve and nine. Although not a great many compared to future sluggers, during the "dead ball" era, when the ball was softer and used more often during the game, this was a mighty accomplishment.

More importantly, it signaled the direction that

Ruppert and Huston wanted to take the team. Ruppert, the more decisive and visionary of the two Yankee owners, knew that fans wanted to see something spectacular at a game, and what could be more spectacular than a towering home run to clear the bases. So Ruppert and Huston went in search of other power hitters.

They found one in 1916 in Frank ("Home Run") Baker, who played for Connie Mack's Philadelphia Athletics. Ruppert and Huston, not afraid to spend a little money, bought Baker's contract for $37,500, even though the 30-year-old third baseman had sat out the 1915 season in a contract dispute with the Athletics' owner.

Baker was a power hitter who, like Pipp, owned a batting title or two, having won or tied the league record for most home runs four seasons in a row prior to 1915. More importantly for Ruppert and Huston, Baker drew a crowd. With Baker in the lineup, attendance nearly doubled overnight. Baker's presence put a spark in the rest of the Yankees, too, and for the first time in years they found themselves in a pennant race.

JOHN FRANKLIN ("HOME RUN")
BAKER played major league baseball from 1908 to 1922, and is regarded as the best third baseman of the pre-war era. Not only an excellent

*infielder, Baker was a strong hitter as well, help-
ing the American League Philadelphia Athletics
win the World Series in 1910, 1911, and 1913.*

*Baker acquired the
nickname "Home
Run" during the 1911
World Series, when he
hit a go-ahead home
run off New York
Giants' pitcher Rube
Marquard in the sec-
ond game of the
series, and a ninth-inning game-tying home run
off Christy Mathewson in the third game. Baker
led the American League in home runs for four
consecutive seasons, from 1911-1914. When he
retired from the Yankees in 1922, Baker had
belted almost 100 career home runs. He was
quickly overshadowed, however, by Yankee teammate Babe Ruth, who hit 113 home runs in his
first two seasons with the Yankees alone.*

But their hopes were dashed when two-thirds into
the 1916 season Baker crashed into the grandstand
chasing a pop fly. Nursing several broken ribs, Baker
sat out the last fifty games of the season. Missing
their star player, the Yankees dropped to fourth place.
But the Yankees were the team to watch.

They continued to struggle through the 1917 season. Donovan, a decent manager and a good man, had more losses than wins, and had brought the team close to the top only once in his three years at the helm. When the Yankees finished the 1917 season in sixth place, 28½ games behind Chicago, Ruppert and Huston fired Donovan.

The process of hiring a new manager, however, proved more difficult than the two owners expected. The difficulty revolved around their choice for the empty position. Huston wanted to hire his friend and drinking buddy, Wilbert Robinson, John McGraw's teammate from the Old Orioles, who was managing the Brooklyn Robins. Ruppert, on the advice of American League president Ban Johnson, wanted to hire Miller ("Mighty Mite") Huggins, a former second baseman, who was managing the St. Louis Cardinals.

Before the two owners could agree, American forces entered World War I and Huston, a colonel in the 18th Engineering Corps, shipped out to France. While Huston was in Europe, Ruppert met with Robinson and Huggins. It was Huggins, who had studied law at the University of Cincinnati, who impressed Ruppert, and he offered Huggins the manager's position on the spot.

When Huston found out that Ruppert had offered Huggins the manager's position without consulting him, he was furious. From his headquarters in France, Huston bombarded Ruppert with cablegrams declaring his outrage. But the cool-eyed, confident Ruppert was not about to bow to Huston's will, and Huggins took the field as the Yankees' new manager.

MILLER JAMES ("MIGHTY MITE") HUGGINS hailed from Cincinnati, the same city in which Ban Johnson began his career as a newspaper editor. Intensely driven and intellectual, Huggins captained the University of Cincinnati's baseball team while completing his law degree. Although he passed the Ohio bar, Huggins chose instead to pursue a career as a professional baseball player, playing semi-professional and minor league baseball until the Cincinnati Reds signed him in 1904. Over the next twelve years, Huggins played second base for the Reds and the St. Louis Cardinals, managing the latter from 1913-1917. The following year he accepted the managing position of the New York Yankees, where he won six American League pennants and three World Series championships before his untimely death at the end of the 1929 season.

In his first full season as manager, Huggins guided the Yankees to a fourth-place finish, even though the team had lost eleven men to the armed forces, including Pipp and Shawkey. The following year, Huggins' Yankees finished the 1919 season in third place behind the mighty Chicago White Sox and a powerful Cleveland team. More importantly, they were starting to show signs that they could hit the long ball, leading the league in home runs with 45 behind the power hitting of Pipp, Baker, shortstop Roger Peckinpaugh, and outfielder Duffy Lewis.

But the Yankees still had a long way to go. Although attendance was up, the New York Giants still pulled in more fans. The Yankees needed another star attraction if they were to increase their gate receipts. With Baker, Pipp, and Lewis aging, Ruppert and Huston, who had returned from Europe, went looking for another marquee, player, a slugger who could belt the ball out of the ballpark.

At the end of the 1919 season, they found their man. His name was George Herman ("Babe") Ruth. Ruth began his baseball career in 1914 playing for Jack Dunn's Baltimore Orioles, at the time a minor league team in the International League. Ruth was a shy, nervous nineteen-year-old who had spent the last eleven years at St. Mary's Industrial School for Boys in Baltimore after his parents had given him up as unmanageable.

Although he stood 6'2" and weighed close to 180 pounds, Ruth acquired the nickname "Babe" partly because of his wide-eyed, innocent-looking baby face, but also because, as he followed Jack Dunn around the Orioles ballpark, some of the veteran players and coaches began referring to him as "Dunnie's Babe." The nickname stuck, and instead of George, or "Jidge" as his St. Mary's teammates called him, his teammates simply called him "Babe."

Although Ruth showed tremendous talent from the beginning, Dunn was more concerned about the survival of his minor league franchise than he was about how Ruth was doing. His worries began at the start of the 1914 season when a third major league, the Federal League, surfaced to challenge the dominance of the American and National Leagues. When the Federal League put a team across the street from Union Park where the Orioles played, attendance for Dunn's minor league team plummeted, and Dunn was forced to sell his best players.

In the middle of the 1914 season, only five months after acquiring the St. Mary's baseball prodigy, Dunn sold Ruth, pitcher Ernie Shore, and catcher Ben Egan to the Boston Red Sox. Reports of the settlement varied, ranging from a high of $25,000 for the trio to a measly $8,500. In any case, Ruth, a rookie fresh out of reform school, was on his way to the majors.

Ruth made his major league debut on July 11, 1914, as a pitcher, beating Cleveland 4-3. But since the Red Sox were not in a race for the American League pennant that year, Red Sox owner Joseph Lannin, who also owned the Providence Grays, sent Ruth to the minor leagues after only two more starts. Ruth played for the Grays, compiling an 8-3 record, good enough to help Providence capture the minor league championship title.

After the minor league season ended, Lannin shipped Ruth back to the Red Sox where he pitched two more times before the end of the 1914 season. That was all of the minor leagues Ruth would ever see. Over the next several years, Ruth became one of major league baseball's best left-handed pitchers, winning 18 games in 1915, 23 games in 1916, and 24 games in 1917, while his earned run average hovered around .200, one of the lowest in the American League. More than that, only two pitchers had more wins and strikeouts. In short, Ruth could pitch.

But he could also hit.

In 1917, Ruth batted .325, a fact that got the attention of Red Sox manager Edward Barrow. In 1918, on the advice of center fielder Harry Hooper, Barrow moved Ruth to the outfield part-time so he could get more at-bats. Although reluctant to take Ruth off the mound completely, Barrow moved Ruth around: he pitched 20 games, played 59 games in the outfield, and covered first base for another 13 games. At the end of the season, Ruth had won 13 games as a pitcher, batted .300, and belted a league-leading 11 home runs.

FOR A BASEBALL MANAGER and front office executive, Edward Grant Barrow was born in a most unlikely place—a covered wagon in Springfield, Illinois. From the start, Barrow had an inherent business sense, working as a soap salesman and ballpark concessionaire as a youth. The latter experience gave him a taste for baseball and he began making his mark in the baseball world, first in the minor leagues (as manager, owner, and league president) and then in the major leagues (as manager and front office executive). As team manager, Barrow led Harry Frazee's Boston Red Sox to a win in the World Series in 1918. Two years later he joined the New York Yankees as their business manager. From 1920 to 1945, Barrow helped the franchise win 14 American League pennants and 10 World Series championships.

The following season, Barrow put Ruth in the outfield for 111 games, using him to pitch only 17 times. It was a wise decision. Ruth batted .322 and led the league in home runs with an incredible 29, almost twice as many as the nearest contender. Not even the entire pennant-winning White Sox hit as many home runs as Ruth did that year.

Ruth, quickly replacing Ty Cobb as the game's most exciting player, was the toast of Boston. It now seemed certain that the Red Sox would continue their streak of pennants and world championship titles, which they had brought to Boston in four of the last eight years. But Ruth's prowess at the plate was not only drawing crowds, it was drawing the attention of other team managers. One of those managers was Miller Huggins.

With the encouragement of Ruppert and Huston, Huggins was slowly putting together a power-hitting team, and Ruth was just what he was looking for. It didn't take long for Huggins to convince the Yankee owners of that either, after all Ruppert and Huston had seen Ruth slug monstrous home runs during spring training and regular season games. Not only was Ruth talented, but he was also a bigger-than-life personality, a headline player if there ever was one.

But it seemed unlikely that the Red Sox would sell Ruth. Ruppert had already half-jokingly made an offer to buy Ruth from the new Red Sox owner, Harry Frazee, who bought the team from Lannin in 1916. Frazee dismissed the offer without batting an eye. The Red Sox were a world-class team, and Ruth was its best player and centerpiece. But that was 1917. This was 1919, and it wasn't a good year for Frazee.

*BABE RUTH AND JOHN MCGRAW, two
key figures in the New York Yankee story stand
together in the photograph below. Now, look*

*closely. Yes,
that's Ruth
(left) decked
out in a New
York Giants'
uniform
standing next
to McGraw,
the feisty,
dictatorial
manager of
the National
League's New York Giants, the Yankees' cross-
town rival. It's a cool day in the fall of 1923.
The two combatants pause long enough to pose
for a photograph during a charity game at the
Polo Grounds.*

*But Ruth in a Giants' uniform isn't that far-
fetched. Not only are both men of Irish-Catholic
descent, but also they both hail from Baltimore.
Why is this important? Because after McGraw
left Baltimore to take the Giants' managerial
position, he still had close ties to key baseball men
in his home city. One of those men was Jack
Dunn, who owned the minor league Baltimore
Orioles.*

It was Dunn who signed Ruth to his first contract. McGraw knew of Ruth as he had seen him play in a game against Newark early in the 1914 season. McGraw offered to buy Ruth for $5000, but Dunn was not ready to sell. After all, Ruth was beginning to draw a crowd when he played at home. But 1914 wasn't a good year for Dunn. A third major league, the Federal League, had just come to town and set up shop right across the street from Dunn's minor league team. Dunn didn't have a chance. From the start the Federal League's team, the Terrapins, syphoned away Dunn's audience.

Halfway through the 1914 season Dunn made a move, only he didn't call McGraw. Dunn knew other baseball men. One of them was Joseph Lannin, who owned two teams: the minor league Providence Grays and the American League's Boston Red Sox. In a historic move, Dunn sold Ruth, catcher Ben Egan, and pitcher Ernie Shore to Lannin. And, as they say, the rest is history. But imagine the story we'd be telling today if Dunn had sold Ruth to the Giants.

You're making a mistake, Harry.
You know that, don't you?
Ed Barrow

CHAPTER SIX

Nothing But Trouble

HARRY FRAZEE'S YEAR began with Ruth demanding a new contract. Frazee had paid Ruth $7,000 for his services in 1918, now Ruth wanted more—a whopping $12,000. Frazee laughed. That was as much money as the greatest players of the era were getting, including pitching ace Cy Young, batting champion Honus Wagner, and all-around great Ty Cobb. But Ruth persisted. He even threatened to retire—to become a boxer, or even an actor.

Frazee was used to actors. He had produced a few Broadway shows, and even owned a theater or two in New York. Yes, Frazee knew actors, and he called Ruth's bluff. In mid-March, Ruth backed down and accepted a three-year contract for $30,000. Even at $10,000 a year, Ruth was still one of the highest paid players in the league.

Ruth should have been satisfied, but he wasn't. Not because of the money, but because Frazee was nagging him about his late night habits. Ruth regularly stayed out all night, often stumbling into his hotel room around five or six in the morning on game days. Frazee wasn't pleased, but Ruth was only one of his problems.

While playing the White Sox in July, Frazee's best right-handed pitcher, Carl Mays, walked off the field during the middle of a game. Mays had been irked by his teammates' lackluster play all season. The final straw came during the team's trip to Chicago when Wally Schang, the Red Sox catcher, beaned Mays on the head trying to throw out a base runner stealing second base. That did it. Partly in disgust, and partly in disbelief, Mays walked off the field, showered, and caught a train back to Boston, leaving word with Ed Barrow, the team's general manager, that he didn't intend to play for Boston again.

When Frazee got word of what happened, instead of disciplining the hard-to-handle Mays for his rash behavior, Frazee turned to Ruppert and Huston and traded the churlish Mays to the Yankees.

When news of the trade reached Johnson, the American League president was furious. If Mays got away with such insubordinate behavior, then any player could do the same, rendering player contracts meaningless. Mays had to be disciplined. Although angry at Frazee for trading Mays, Johnson aimed his displeasure at New York Yankee owners Ruppert and Huston who had bought Mays' contract. Johnson ordered the owners not to play Mays until he could review the case fully. Never fond of Johnson's constant meddling in the affairs of league owners, Ruppert and Huston appealed Johnson's order. But Johnson held firm.

CARL MAYS made his Major League pitching debut with the Boston Red Sox in 1915, the same year Babe Ruth joined the club full time. Mays spent fifteen years in the major leagues playing for four teams: the Red Sox, the New York Yankees, the Cincinnati Reds, and the New York Giants. Surly and ill-tempered, Mays was known around the league as a "head hunter" (a pitcher who threw at a batter on purpose). His reputation for head hunting became cemented while pitching for the Yankees. On August 16, 1920, while pursuing his 100th career win, Mays let loose one of his signature high-and-inside submarine pitches, hitting Ray Chapman of the Cleveland Indians in the head. Chapman died

from the injury the following day, and remains the only major league player to die from being hit by a pitch. For all his surliness, however, Mays was effective, compiling a 207-126 win-loss record and an impressive 2.92 earned run average.

Ruppert and Huston, who had never fully pledged their allegiance to Johnson, went to court to get an injunction to restrain Johnson from interfering. When the lower court ruled in favor of the Yankee owners, Johnson appealed to the New York Supreme Court. The judge who took the case, however, ruled in favor of the Yankees, issuing a permanent injunction that barred Johnson from interfering with the Mays trade.

Now, the battle lines were drawn. Frazee, Ruppert, Huston, and Comiskey (once Johnson's closest ally) squared off against Johnson, Garry Herrmann, president of the National League's Cincinnati Reds and chairman of the three-man National Commission, and five American League owners who remained loyal to Johnson.

The disagreement between the two factions was not the only tension in Frazee's life however. He was hurting financially as well. Not only had the war-shortened 1918 season cut into his profits (both his baseball and theatrical profits), but also former Red

Sox owner Joseph Lannin was suing Frazee for $125,000, the amount Frazee supposedly still owed Lannin as part of the original sale of the Red Sox in 1916. Although the two men eventually settled out of court for an undisclosed amount, Frazee's year was marked with nothing but trouble. And more trouble was around the corner.

At the end of the 1919 season, Ruth demanded more money, even though he had signed a three-year contract at the beginning of the season. Ruth wanted twice as much as he made in 1919—an astronomical $20,000 a year. Frazee had had enough, and he let it be known that he was willing to sell Ruth. But by 1919, Frazee's options were limited since he had formed a union with Ruppert, Huston and Comiskey against Johnson, Herrmann, and the rest of the American League owners. Realistically, Frazee had only two options, if he wanted to maintain his alliance with Ruppert, Huston and Comiskey: he could trade Ruth to New York, or he could trade him to Chicago.

Comiskey's White Sox were the best team in baseball, even though Cincinnati had upset them in the 1919 World Series (which later became one of major league baseball's biggest scandals when it was learned that several White Sox players had conspired to throw the series). Trading with Comiskey was tricky. Frazee didn't want to strengthen their hand any more than he could help it. Besides, Frazee was a New

Yorker and knew the Yankee owners personally. More importantly, Ruppert and Huston had money to burn.

So, when the Yankee owners approached Frazee at the end of the 1919 season to see if the Red Sox owner would sell Ruth, Frazee was receptive. On December 26, 1919, the day after Christmas, Frazee settled with the Yankee owners. Ruppert and Huston bought Ruth for $100,000 (though interest on the payment schedule brought the figure closer to $125,000). In addition, Ruppert personally loaned Frazee $350,000, secured by a mortgage on Fenway Park, the Red Sox's home ballfield.

With the deal finalized, now all the Yankee owners had to do was to convince Ruth, who was in California playing exhibition games. Huggins was dispatched for the job. After some haggling, Ruth agreed to a two-year contract at $20,000 a year, the same amount he had demanded of Frazee several months earlier. In addition, Ruth received a $1,000 signing bonus. Ruth was now the highest-paid ballplayer in either league, making four or five times that of the average player.

Ruth foreshadowed his greatness by hitting his first home run as a Yankee clear out of the Polo Grounds, a feat he accomplished only three times in his career. By year's end, Ruth had clobbered 54 home runs, more than twice that of any other player. He was also number one in runs batted in and runs scored, and his slugging percentage was a whopping .847. Ruth's jump in home-run output between 1919 and 1920, from 29 to 54 home runs, was also a sign of the times. The "dead ball" era, which characterized major league baseball from its inception, was coming to an end. One of the reasons was how baseballs were made.

Prior to 1910, baseballs were fashioned by winding woolen thread around a solid wood center, which was then wrapped in a leather covering. In 1910, the Spalding Company, which supplied the major leagues with baseballs, began experimenting with a new rubber-encased cork center. In 1919, they made one more adjustment: they introduced a higher quality woolen thread that wound much tighter around the cork-and-rubber center. This made the ball harder and much more "lively" when hit.

THE FIRST BASEBALLS were nothing more than a long piece of string wrapped tightly around a firm center (a wood chip, a walnut, a pebble, etc.). Good for amateurs, but not professionals. The first professional baseballs had cushioned wooden cores patented by Albert Spalding in the late 19th century. In 1910, major league baseball adopted the cork-centered baseball patented by Philadelphia Athletics president Ben Shibe. During World War II, rubber centers were used due to wartime restrictions on the domestic use of cork.

Today, a baseball starts as a small sphere of cork encased in a rubber shell. The resultant sphere, or "pill" as it is called, is tightly wound with several layers of wool yarn, with one last winding of cotton or polyester yarn. The final core is coated with latex adhesive, which turns the sphere into a gooey but hard lump, which is then fitted with a tight-fitting jacket of leather (originally horsehide, but now cowhide).

The leather jacket is hand-stitched with 108 double stitches using a waxed red cotton thread. After a wooden press rolls the seams flat, the ball is stored in a dehumidifying room that shrinks the cover tight. A baseball bound for the major leagues, which must weigh between 5 and 5¼ ounces and be 9 to 9¼ inches in circumference, is not ready for use until the Commissioner of Baseball's signature is stamped onto it.

Not only were balls livelier, but new balls were also put into play more often. The result was immediate: between 1920 and 1925, home runs increased by 350 percent. Baseball strategy changed as well. In the hit-happy game of the "live ball" era, teams relied on the big inning where a burst of hits, capped by a home run or two, produced enough runs to keep a team ahead for the remainder of the game (unless, of course, the opposing team had one or two big innings as well).

This was the world that Ruth stepped into. But this is not to say that he didn't have natural hitting abilities all his own. He still stood head and shoulders above the rest of the players when it came to hitting the long ball. In this regard, he was a one-man show, though with a fine supporting cast, many of whom Ruppert and Huston purchased from Frazee's Red Sox. Within a four-year period, from 1919 to 1923, Frazee sold a dozen or more players to Ruppert and Huston, including pitchers Waite Hoyt, Harry Harper, Herb Pennock, Joe Bush, and Sam Jones, catcher Wally Schang, infielders Everett Scott, Joe Dugan, and Mike McNally, and outfielder Elmer Smith, not to mention submariner Carl Mays and slugger Babe Ruth.

Now, the Yankees were poised to win. And they did, taking their first American League pennant in 1921, finishing four-and-a-half games ahead of Cleveland. Ruth claimed his third straight home run title, belting an incredible 59 home runs, enough to propel the Yankees ahead of all other teams with a total of 134 home runs. Along with Yankee hitting, Ruth had the help of two former Red Sox pitchers, Mays and Hoyt, who won 46 games between them, with Mays leading the league with 27 wins.

Their next challenge was a shot at McGraw's

New York Giants for the world championship title. McGraw was now co-owner of the Giants, having bought into the franchise at the beginning of the 1919 season when a syndicate headed by Charles Stoneham bought the Giants from Brush's heirs.

With Mays and Hoyt on the mound, the Yankees won the first two games easily, blanking the Giants in both games 3-0. Ruth, getting mostly walks from the Giants' pitching staff, made several colorful steals. On one of the steals, Ruth slammed into the bag, badly scraping his elbow. In the third game, the Yankees ran up the score quickly, 4-0, but after twenty scoreless innings the Giants managed to tie the game in the third inning, and then went on to win easily, 13-5. Ruth stole another base, but in doing so he re-injured his elbow.

("Sad") Sam Jones, ("Bullet") Joe Bush, and Everett ("The Deacon") Scott pose for a photograph in 1922 with their new team, the New York Yankees.

The Giants won the fourth game, tying the series two games apiece, but it was a memorable game for Ruth, who hit his first World Series home run in the ninth inning. The Yankees prevailed in the fifth game, beating the Giants 3-1, partly on a surprising play by Ruth. After striking out in the first inning, Ruth bunted in the fourth inning for a single; then scored on a double by teammate Bob Meusel.

That was the last hurrah for Ruth and the Yankees. Due to his injured elbow, which had become infected, Ruth didn't dress for the next two games, which the Yankees lost. Although he was back in uniform for the seventh game of the series, Ruth didn't play until Yankee manager Miller Huggins put him in as a pinch-hitter in the ninth inning. Ruth grounded out and the Giants went on to win the game and the series five games to three.

GEORGE HERMAN ("BABE") RUTH
honed his baseball skills at St. Mary's Industrial

School for Boys in Baltimore. After playing half a season for the minor league Baltimore Orioles, Ruth was sold to the Boston Red Sox. In 1919, Ruth was sold again, to the New York Yankees where he quickly became known for his towering home runs and larger-than-life personality.

The Yankees opened the 1922 season without Ruth, but not because of his injured elbow. It was Ruth's bad judgment, something that got him into trouble throughout his career. After the 1921 season, Ruth and teammates Bob Meusel and Bill Piercy went on a post-season barnstorming tour against the advice of Judge Kenesaw Mountain Landis, the newly appointed Commissioner of Baseball.

In trying to bring some respectability to the game after the notorious Black Sox scandal, Landis prohibited players who had played in the World Series from participating in post-season barnstorming or exhibition games. Such games were an integral part of major league baseball. Not only did they promote professional baseball in out-of-the-way places, but they also provided players additional revenue, an important supplement to their salary.

The problem with post-season games as Landis saw it was that the teams that went on the tours were rarely representative of the pennant-winning teams, which they often billed themselves as. At best, only two or three players of the pennant-winning teams went on the tour, the rest of the team stocked by mediocre fill-ins. Landis thought that they were shams and only devalued the post-season championship series. Club owners, too, were skeptical of post-season games, which they argued took away from their own pre-season exhibition games.

With this in mind, Landis prohibited players of World Series teams from participating in post-season barnstorming tours. But Ruth, Meusel, and Piercy thumbed their nose at Landis and went anyway. As a result, Landis not only fined the three players for insubordinate behavior, but he also suspended them for the first six weeks of the 1922 season.

When he finally got a chance to play, the still-smarting Ruth hit 35 home runs by season's end, prodding his Yankee teammates on to their second straight American League pennant, though by a margin of only one game over the red-hot St. Louis Browns.

McGraw's Giants, however, were waiting for the upstart American League pennant winners, thrashing the Yankees soundly as they swept the series four games to none. Curiously, it was the only World Series in which a game was called on account of darkness. In the second game, with the score tied 2-2, the umpires called the game in the tenth inning.

Despite the fact that the Giants had beaten the Yankees in two straight world championship series, McGraw was not happy. The source of his unhappiness came from the fact that fans flocked to the Polo Grounds not to see his world champion New York Giants; they came to witness the Herculean feats of Yankee slugger Babe Ruth. McGraw would take care of that, or so he thought.

In the spring of 1921, McGraw, with the support of Giants' owner Charles Stoneham, informed Ruppert and Huston that their lease at the Polo Grounds would not be renewed. It was a strategic decision: the Yankees without a ballpark would have to pack up and move, probably to some distant New York City borough or, better yet, to the farmlands of New Jersey.

Anticipating this, the Yankee owners were already looking for a suitable place to build a stadium of their own. First, they looked at a piece of property on Long Island, but it was rejected. Then, they made an offer on property in upper Manhattan owned by the Hebrew Orphan Asylum, but the offer fell through. They even considered constructing a stadium over the Pennsylvania Railroad tracks in downtown Manhattan. But that plan was scrapped, too.

Finally, much to McGraw's consternation, Ruppert and Huston settled on a plot of land in the Bronx, a mere stone's throw across the Harlem River from the Polo Grounds.

Every day I want to win ten to nothing.
Jake Ruppert

CHAPTER SEVEN

Ruppert's Palace

THE PROPERTY LOCATED between 158th and 161st Streets on River Avenue was a 10-acre plot of land owned by the estate of the William Waldorf Astor. Ruppert and Huston bought the land, a former lumberyard clogged with debris, for $600,000. Prior to being a lumberyard, it was a prime piece of farmland.

The original plan for the new stadium was drawn up by the Osborn Engineering Company of Cleveland, which had designed a number of other major league ballparks including Comiskey Park, Griffith Stadium, and Tiger Stadium, to name a few. The innovative plan called for a continuous grandstand to encircle the field. But the need for more natural light, and the great expense, prohibited such a design. Ruppert and Huston settled instead on an open, oval-shaped stadium with a sheltered grandstand that wrapped around home plate. The oval design would distinguish it from its neighbor, the Polo Grounds, which was built in the shape of a perfect horseshoe.

The White Construction Company of New York was contracted to build the stadium on the promise that they would have the stadium built in time for the 1923 season, less than a year away. Work began the first week of May 1922. The first job entailed clearing the property of debris, and then grading the land with over 45,000 cubic yards of earth (on top of which 13,000 cubic yards of top soil would be dumped). Once this was completed, construction on the stadium could begin.

The steel-and-concrete structure, with its first-ever triple-deck grandstand, was designed to seat 58,000 fans, 6,000 more fans than the Polo Grounds, which had been rebuilt after the 1911 fire, increasing its capacity from 40,000 to 52,000 seats. To construct the grandstand, over three million board feet of temporary formwork was required, into which 20,000 cubic yards of concrete would be poured. The seats in the grandstand, manufactured on site, required 135,000 individual steel castings, to which 40,000 pieces of maple lumber were secured with over one million brass screws.

In short, it would be a massive structure, known to New Yorkers as "The House that Ruth Built," a phrase attributed to sportswriter Fred Lieb of the *New York Evening Telegram*. To Ruppert's closest friends, however, it was known as "Ruppert's Palace." Huston, who never forgave Ruppert for hiring Miller Huggins over Wilbert Robinson, took less and less of an active role in managing the Yankees, finally selling his interest in the franchise for a reported $1.25 million to Ruppert before the start of the 1923 season (though staying on as a member of the Board of Directors).

Along with its massive size—and cost (an estimated $2.5 million)—several other features distinguished the stadium, including an enormous electronic scoreboard, the first of its kind, in right center field, and a 16-foot-high scalloped copper frieze that capped the grandstand roof, giving the stadium its signature Greco-Roman or "classical" look. The most curious addition, however, was the brick-lined vault buried 15 feet beneath second base that housed telephone, telegraph and other electrical equipment used by the press when the stadium hosted title boxing matches.

The playing field was also memorable. While the right-field line measured 296 feet (with a low fence to accommodate Ruth's southpaw stroke), and the left-field line came in at 281 feet, center field, known as "Death Valley," was a graveyard for hitters, stretching a seemingly endless 500 feet to the fence.

Despite worker strikes and layoffs, the White Construction Company kept its word and completed construction in time for opening day, in a blinding 284 days.

The new stadium opened on April 18, 1923. It was a typical spring day in New York—cold and blustery. But just as the weather was brisk, so, too, was business at Yankee Stadium. Fans arrived by the thousands and by a variety of means: by car, by bike, by foot, by train, by any means possible. (Commissioner Landis came by subway, eschewing any fan that took a taxi to the ballgame.)

According to local newspaper accounts, close to 74,000 fans crammed into the new stadium for the inaugural game (though the official count put it closer to 62,000), while another 25,000, who were turned away at the gates, milled around outside, hoping to get a glimpse of the action inside the ballpark.

A festive atmosphere greeted those who entered the stadium by the front entrance. The Stars-and-Stripes waved atop the stadium façade and fluttered over the entrance gates in a series of patriotic displays. Inside, flag bunting decorated the grandstand. Every New Yorker of note was there: Governor Al Smith and his wife, Baseball Commissioner Kenesaw Mountain Landis, Police Commissioner Richard Enright, New York Giants' owner Charles Stoneham, Boston Red Sox owner Harry Frazee, and, of course,

Miller Huggins and Frank Chance hoist the "Stars-and-Stripes" in deep center field at the opening of Yankee Stadium on April 18, 1923, while bandmaster John Philip Sousa conducts the Seventh Regiment Band playing "The Star-Spangled Banner."

Yankee owners Jake Ruppert and T. L. Huston. The only noticeable absences were New York City Mayor John Hylan, who was in bed with a cold, and American League president Ban Johnson.

The permanent injunction that the New York Supreme Court issued against Johnson barring him from interfering with the Carl Mays' trade in the middle of the 1919 season was not the end of the tension between Johnson and his supporters, and Frazee, Ruppert and Huston.

By coincidence, Frazee, Ruppert and Comiskey were serving rotating terms on the American League's three-member Board of Directors. In their capacity as league representatives, they called for Johnson to resign, contending that Johnson's long-term contract as American League president was invalid, since Johnson had forced the contract on club owners when the league was formed in 1901. The trio of club owners also threatened to withdraw from the league and form a new league with teams from the National League if Johnson didn't step down as league president.

Since Johnson still had the support of a majority of club owners, he turned a deaf ear to their threats. Within weeks, at the American League's annual midwinter meeting in 1920, Johnson and his supporters voted to oust the "insurrectionists" (which Johnson had dubbed Frazee, Ruppert and Comiskey) from the league's Board of Directors.

Johnson didn't stop there. He withheld money the Yankees should have received from the American League for their 1919 third place finish. This action infuriated Ruppert and Huston who, after paying their ballplayers out of their own pockets, filed a lawsuit against Johnson and his followers.

When American League officials met again in Chicago after the first of the year, Johnson's supporters, unnerved by the lawsuits, broke ranks with Johnson. They voted to reinstate Mays, gave the Yankees their third-place money, and established a two-year arbitration committee, consisting of Ruppert and Clark Griffith, who owned the Washington Senators, to review all of Johnson's disciplinary decisions. In addition, Johnson agreed to drop his claim that he had been given a lifetime contract as league president.

In return, Ruppert and Huston dropped their lawsuits against Johnson and his supporters. But the damage had been done: Johnson's absolute power over professional baseball had been broken. It was further weakened when Johnson failed to act on rumors he received that the 1919 World Series had been thrown by members of the Chicago White Sox. When the "Black Sox" scandal finally broke in September of 1920, and eight White Sox players were indicted for throwing the series, Johnson's credibility was at an all-time low.

Frazee, Comiskey and Ruppert wasted no time and called for the elimination of the three-man National Commission, of which Johnson was a founding member. At the same time, they campaigned for the establishment of an independent Commissioner of Baseball, an idea that Frazee had been circulating for several years, ever since the war-shortened 1918 season when Frazee argued, against Johnson's wishes, for a longer season than the War Department wanted to allow.

The idea of replacing the National Commission with a single Commissioner of Baseball was extreme, and Johnson and his supporters balked. But Frazee, Ruppert and Comiskey once again threatened to walk out and form a new league if they didn't comply with their demands. Caught in the middle of the bitter dispute, club owners agreed with the trio and appointed

Opening Day, Yankee Stadium, April 18, 1923. From left to right: Jake Ruppert, co-owner New York Yankees, Kenesaw Mountain Landis, Commissioner of Baseball, T. L. Huston, co-owner New York Yankees, and Harry Frazee, owner Boston Red Sox.

Judge Kenesaw Mountain Landis, a federal judge in Northern Illinois, the first Commissioner of Baseball.

And so, on opening day, it was Landis—not Johnson—who led dignitaries to deep center field for the flag-raising ceremonies. The overflow crowd was respectful, even quiet, as the Seventh Regiment Band, under the direction of John Philip Sousa, played *The Star-Spangled Banner*. But when the Yankees' pennant of 1922 was hoisted, the crowd let loose a tumultuous roar.

After Governor Al Smith threw out the first pitch, the Yankees took the field against Harry Frazee's Boston Red Sox. It was a close game, until the third inning. With the game tied 1-1, Ruth stepped up to the plate. He had hoped to hit the first home run in the first game in the new stadium, even half-heartedly promising to give a year of his life if he did so.

He got his wish.

With two men on base, Ruth smacked a towering home run into the right-field stands, a section of the ballpark that would forever be known as "Ruthville." With the crowd cheering wildly, and Ruppert and Huston beaming, Ruth circled the bases, taking in all of the sights and sounds of the day. Then, as he soft-stepped across home plate, the Yankee slugger doffed his cap and waved to the crowd. Yankee Stadium was officially christened, and who better to christen it than the mighty Babe Ruth.

The Yankees went on to finish the season with their best winning percentage, claiming their third American League pennant in as many years, some 16 games ahead of Detroit. Ruth, too, had a good year. He batted a team-leading .393, and also led his teammates in hits (205), doubles (45), triples (13), and even stolen bases (17). But more than that, he led the American League in home runs (41), runs batted in (131), and total runs scored (151).

Ruth was Mr. Baseball. Not only was he the most powerful hitter of his day, but he was also the most popular player on and off the field. Thus, when it came time to play the World Series, expectations were high for the Yankees, no longer seen as an upstart team, but a true contender for the championship title.

To win, however, they had to beat John McGraw's New York Giants, still major league baseball's most powerful team. But the Yankees were no longer McGraw's tenants at the Polo Grounds. They were their own team, playing in their own stadium, attracting their own fans (which had swelled to more than a million a year, topping all other American League records). Although the Giants had won the last two World Series match-ups, sweeping a humiliated Yankee team the previous year, the Yankees were a confident, hard-playing, hungry team.

Even so, it would not be an easy battle.

The two teams seemed perfectly matched, alternating wins for the first four games. In game five, with the series tied at two apiece, the Yankees took the lead with an 8-1 win behind the pitching of Joe Bush. Now the Yankees only needed one more win in the best-of-seven series to be crowned major league baseball's champions. They got it with strong pitching from Herb Pennock and Sam Jones, and a pivotal home run by Ruth, his third of the series, a new World Series record.

But it was Ruth's two home runs in the second game that were key to the Yankees' success. Prior to game two, the Giants had taken eight consecutive wins over the Yankees in post-season play. Ruth's two home runs not only lifted the Yankees over the Giants after losing the first game, but they also boosted the Yankees' confidence that they could beat their cross-town rival for the championship title. And they did, winning the last three games of the series for a 4-2 edge over the Giants.

The Yankees had finally arrived. They had weathered the humiliation of the Hilltop Highlander years. They had overcome the scorn and ridicule of New York Giants' owners Andrew Freedman and John Brush. They had outwitted the feisty and conniving John McGraw, the Giants' fearless manager. Moreover, they had endured the wrath of American League president Ban Johnson. Now, finally, the Yankees stood atop the baseball world as champions.

World Champions!

It would be a place they would stand often. No other franchise in the history of organized baseball would win as many league pennants and World Series championship titles as the New York Yankees. No wonder Ruppert would boast at a lavish celebration at the Commodore Hotel in downtown Manhattan after the 1923 World Series: "This is the happiest day of my life! Now I have baseball's greatest park and baseball's greatest team!"

And he did.

TODAY, MANY FANS who attend a game at Yankee Stadium take time to visit Monument Park, which anyone can do up to a half hour before the first pitch. The park, located beyond the outfield fence in dead center, is filled with monuments, plaques, and retired player uniforms, honoring some of the greatest members of the Yankee organization.

But Monument Park, the area's official name, didn't start as a dedicated space outside the playing field. It started with one lone monument in the far reaches of centerfield, which at the time was almost 500 feet deep.

To honor the memory of team manager Miller Huggins, who died suddenly at the end of the 1929 season, Yankee owner Jake Ruppert had a free-standing monument erected in Huggins' honor in front of the flagpole in deep center. The monument, made to resemble a headstone, consisted of a bronze plaque mounted on an upright block of red granite.

By 1950, two other monuments had been erected: one to honor first baseman and team captain Lou Gehrig; another to honor slugger Babe Ruth. Over time a number of smaller plaques honoring other members of the Yankee organization were mounted on the outfield wall behind the original three monuments.

The monument area became separate from the playing field during stadium renovations in the mid-1970s when the centerfield fence was moved in 44 feet. Although it was not until 1985 that the public was given access to the area, which now contained the original flagpole, the wall-mounted plaques, and five monuments (two more were added: one to honor Mickey Mantle; another to honor Joe DiMaggio). It was around this time that Monument Park got its official name, becoming an integral part of the fans' experience of Yankee Stadium.

When a completely remodeled Yankee Stadium opened its doors in 2009 across the street from the old ballpark, a replica Monument Park was built beyond centerfield fence, containing the contents of the old park in addition to new plaques and retired player numbers. It also included the New York Yankee logo set in black marble and a small September 11th monument.

Although the Yankee organization has grown over time, and can now point to dozens of individuals who have contributed to the success of the organization, still, when it comes down to it, there was just a handful of men—many of them friends, but just as often adversaries—who made the Yankees the team and the organization they are today.

SOURCES

Ghosts from the Past

Baseball is a... Albert Spalding, major league pitcher, manager, owner, National League president, and sporting goods magnate. Source: *Baseball Almanac* www.baseball-almanac.com/quotes/quospld.shtml

Waiting in the Wings

A good umpire... Ban Johnson, founder and president of the American League. Source: *Baseball Almanac* www.baseball-almanac.com/quotes/quojhns2.shtml

Double-crossed

With my team... John McGraw, manager, New York Giants. Source: *Baseball Almanac* www.baseball-almanac.com/quotes/quomcg2.shtml

*Connie Mack's Code...*Connie Mack, owner, Philadelphia Athletics. Source: James, Bill. *The Bill James Guide to Baseball Managers.* New York: Scribner, 1997, p. 63.

New York at Last

Keep your eye... Willie Keeler's response to reporter Abe Yager of the *Brooklyn Eagle* when asked about his hitting ability. Source: Appel, Marty. *Pinstripe Nation: The New York Yankees from Before the Babe to After the Boss.* New York: Bloomsbury, 2012, p. 23.

The brightest spot... how the *New York Times* characterized Frank Chase, the Yankees' new manager in 1913. Source: Appel, Marty. *Pinstripe Nation: The New York Yankees from Before the Babe to After the Boss.* New York: Bloomsbury, 2012, p. 59.

Looking for a Plaything

A good manager... Miller Huggins, manager, New York Yankees. Source: *Baseball Almanac:* www.baseball-almanac.com/quotes/quohugg.shtml

Nothing But Trouble

You're making a... Red Sox manager Ed Barrow to Red Sox owner Harry Frazee upon learning of Frazee's decision to sell Babe Ruth to the Yankees. Source: Appel, Marty. *Pinstripe Nation: The New York Yankees from Before the Babe to After the Boss.* New York: Bloomsbury, 2012, p. 96.

Ruppert's Palace

Every day I... Jake Ruppert, owner, New York Yankees, after the Yankees won their first World Series title in 1923. Source: Abruzzese, Rob. *Bronx Baseball Daily*, www.bronxbaseballdaily.com/2011/05/classic-yankees-jacob-ruppert

*The house that...*attributed to Fred Lieb, reporter, *New York Evening Telegram.* Source: Montville, Leigh. *The Big Bam: The Life and Times of Babe Ruth.* New York: Broadway Books, 2006, p. 174.

This is a... Jake Ruppert, owner, New York Yankees, at the Hotel Commodore celebrating the New York Yankees' first World Series title. Source: Wagenheim, Kal. *Babe Ruth: His Life and Legend.* New York: Praeger, 1974, p. 137.

BIBLIOGRAPHY

Alexander, Charles C. *John McGraw*. New York: Viking, 1988.

Antonucci, Thomas J. and Eric Caren. *Big League Baseball in the Big Apple: The New York Yankees*. Verplank, New York: Historical Briefs, 1995.

Appel, Marty. *Pinstripe Nation: The New York Yankees from Before the Babe to After the Boss*. New York: Bloomsbury, 2012.

Bjarkman, Peter C. *Encyclopedia of Major League Baseball Team Histories: American League*. Westport, CT: Meckler, 1991.

Chadwick, Dean. *Those Damn Yankees: The Secret Life of America's Greatest Franchise*. New York: Verso, 1999.

Creamer, Robert. *Babe: The Legend Comes to Life*. New York: Simon & Schuster, 1974.

Frommer, Harvey. *A Yankee Century*. New York: Berkley, 2002.

_____. *Big Apple Baseball*. Dallas: Taylor Publishing Company, 1995.

_____. *The New York Yankee Encyclopedia*. New York: Mountain Lion, 1997.

Gallagher, Mark and Walter LeConte. *The Yankee Encyclopedia*. 4th edition. Champaign, IL: Sports Publishers, Inc., 2000.

Gentile, Derek. *The Complete New York Yankees: The Total Encyclopedia of the Team*. New York: Black Dog & Leventhal, 2001.

Gershman, Michael. *Diamond: The Evolution of the Ballpark*. Boston: Houghton Mifflin, 1993.

Hampton, Wilborn. *Up Close: Babe Ruth*. New York: Viking, 2009.

Honig, Donald. *The New York Yankees*. Revised edition. New York: Crown, 1987.

Istorico, Ray. *Greatness in Waiting: An Illustrated History of the Early New York Yankees, 1903-1919*. Jefferson, NC: McFarland, 2008.

James, Bill. *The Bill James Guide to Baseball Managers*. New York: Scribner, 1997.

Keene, Kerry, Raymond Sinibaldi and David Hickey. *The Babe in Red Stockings*. Champaign, IL: Sagamore Publishing, 1997.

Kohout, Martin. *Hal Chase: The Defiant Life and Turbulent Times of Baseball's Biggest Crook*. Jefferson, NC: McFarland, 2001.

Koppett, Leonard. *Koppett's Concise History of Major League Baseball*. Philadelphia: Temple University Press, 1998.

Linn, Ed. *The Great Rivalry: The Yankees and the Red Sox, 1901-1990*. New York: Ticknor & Fields, 1991.

Luisi, Vincent. *New York Yankees: The First 25 Years*. Charleston, SC: Arcadia Publishing, 2002.

Mayer, Ronald A.. *The 1923 New York Yankees*. Jefferson, NC: McFarland, 2010.

Montville, Leigh. *The Big Bam*. New York: Doubleday, 2006.

Murdock, Eugene C. *Ban Johnson: Czar of Baseball*. Westport, CT: Greenwood Press, 1982.

Okrent, Daniel and Harris Lewine. *The Ultimate Baseball Book.* Boston: Houghton Mifflin, 1988.

Patterson, Ted. *The Baltimore Orioles.* Dallas, TX: Taylor Publishing, 2000.

Pepe, Phil. *The Yankees: The Authorized History of the New York Yankees.* Dallas: Taylor Publishing, 1998.

Rains, Rob. *Rawlings Presents Big Stix: The Greatest Hitters in the History of the Major Leagues.* Sports Publishing, Champaign, IL, 2004.

Reisler, Jim. *Babe Ruth: Launching the Legend.* New York: McGraw-Hill, 2004.

_____. *Before They Were the Bombers: The New York Yankees Early Years, 1903-1915.* Jefferson, NC: McFarland, 2002.

Ritter, Lawrence. *The Babe: A Life in Pictures.* New York: Ticknor & Fields, 1988.

Robinson, Ray and Christopher Jennison. *Yankee Stadium: 75 Years of Drama, Glamor, and Glory.* New York: Penguin Studio, 1998.

Ruth, Babe and Bob Considine. *The Babe Ruth Story.* New York: E. P. Dutton & Co., 1948.

Solomon, Burt. *Where They Ain't*. New York: The Free Press, 1999.

Sparks, Barry. *Frank "Home Run" Baker*. Jefferson, NC: McFarland, 2006.

Spatz, Lyle. *Yankees Coming, Yankees Going: New York Yankee Player Transactions, 1903 Through 1999*. Jefferson, NC: McFarland, 2000.

Spatz, Lyle, and Steve Steinberg. *1921: The Yankees, the Giants, and the Battle for Baseball Supremacy in New York*. Lincoln, NE: University of Nebraska Press, 1910.

Stout, Glenn. *Yankees Century: 100 Years of New York Yankees Baseball*. Boston: Houghton Mifflin Harcourt, 2002.

Sullivan, George, and John Powers. *The Yankees: An Illustrated History*. Philadelphia: Temple University Press, 1997.

Thornley, Stew. *Land of the Giants*. Philadelphia: Temple University Press, 2000.

Tygiel, Jules. *Pastime: Baseball as History*. New York: Oxford University Press, 2000.

Vancil, Mark, and Mark Mandrake. *One Hundred Years: New York Yankees: The Official Retrospective.* New York: Ballantine, 2002.

Wagenheim, Kal. *Babe Ruth: His Life and Legend.* New York: Praeger, 1974.

Ward, Geoffrey C. & Ken Burns. *Baseball: An Illustrated History.* New York: Knopf, 1994.

Weintraub, Robert. *The House That Ruth Built.* New York: Little, Brown and Company/Hachette Book Group, 2011.

White, G. Edward. *Creating the National Pastime: Baseball Transforms Itself, 1903-1953.* Princeton, NJ: Princeton University Press, 1996.

INTERNET RESOURCES

The Internet is an invaluable resource for any researcher. Here are a few sites I found particularly helpful in researching this book:

www.aafla.org
www.baseball-almanac.com
www.baseball-links.com
www.baseballhalloffame.org
www.baseballlibrary.com
www.hardballtimes.com
www.majorleaguebaseball.com
www.pinstripedbible.com
www.sabr.org
www.thedeadballera.com
www.yankeeclassic.com

PHOTO CREDITS

All photographs courtesy of the George Grantham Bain Collection, Library of Congress. The Bain Collection represents the photographic files of one of America's earliest news picture agencies. The collection richly documents sports events, theater, celebrities, crime, strikes, disasters, and political activities. The photographs Bain produced and gathered for distribution through his news service were worldwide in their coverage, but there was a special emphasis on life in New York City, with the bulk of the collection dating from the early 1900s to the mid-1920s.

INDEX OF NAMES

ABOUT THE AUTHOR

W. Nikola-Lisa is a freelance author with over 20 books to his credit, including the best-selling *Bein' With You This Way* and *Shake Dem Halloween Bones* for the young reader and *How We Are Smart* and *Dragonfly: A Childhood Memoir* for the older reader. The idea for *The Men Who Made the Yankees* came from work on an earlier book by the author: *Dear Frank: Babe Ruth, the Red Sox, and the Great War.* Learn more about the author and his work at nikolabooks.com and gyroscopebooks.com.

CPSIA information can be obtained
at www.ICGtesting.com
Printed in the USA
LVOW04*2157130416
483538LV00010B/60/P